KU-264-932

With special thanks to Beverley Minster
Church of England Primary School, Burdett Coutts and
Townshend Primary School, and Notting Hill
and Ealing High School (Junior Department)

Trixie

very extremely Brilliant guide to everything

ROS ASQUITH

HarperCollins *Children's Books*

Hi, it's me, Trixie, again – your bestest friend ever. (Well, that's what it says on the covers of my books, so it must be true.) This book you are about to read is a GUIDE – not the girls in uniform, "promise on my honour to do my best" variety – but a book on almost everything you need to know about Tweenage Life in the 21st Century. Tweenage Life, by the way, is what I call that funny bit of life in between when you're a little kid who likes Barbies and when you get to turn into a real live teenager and can start howling at the moon and leaving your socks all over the floor and shouting at your parents. That will be fun, I bet. But Tweenage Life is even more fun. You get to do almost everything: you can tie your laces and go on a bus and do Halloween and all that stuff, but you've got no worries! No responsibilities! (Well, quite a lot of worries and responsibilities actually, but I'll show you how to make them much less.)

In this fantastic and amazingly cheap book you will find the answers to life's great questions, such as: where do all the socks go? And why do teachers get tea and biscuits while we all queue for the water fountain?

The good bit is, you don't have to read it all! You can just hop and skip about as you like. But, say you've got a really big anxiety like: what if I wet the bed staying at the sleepover? (Gulp.) Well, just zoom along to B for bed-wetting. Brilliant isn't it? I hope you are not throwing this book away and saying, "Huh. Wetting the bed is only for little kids," because you would be wrong, as it is actually quite common. I also hope you are not thinking, "This is only for girls, because it is written by a girl." I think boys and girls are quite alike, as it happens, although they do seem to get very strangely different at about twelve, which is a result apparently, of things called hormones which whizz around your body and turn you into a grown-up. Funny to think that one day ALL the girls in my class will have a bra! (I don't mean to say they will all share the same one, they will have one or two each, of course),

The Attack of the Giant Bra

but that time is yet to come, for most of us. I think it may be rather a long time for me, as I look annoyingly about six years old, although this isn't always annoying as it is very good for getting out of trouble. Heh! Heh!

So, dear readers, here begins my AMAZING ALPHABETIC GUIDE – an A-Z of all the Things you ever wanted to know about. Everything – except really boring stuff like how cement is made and whether we get wool from sheep or cows. If you want to know that stuff you can go to a teacher. Teachers love it if you ask a nice question like,

"Please Miss, how did the Tudors roast their oxes?" or something.

Now I will blow a big fanfare thingy on my trumpet (I love to play the trumpet and so would you) and my best friends Dinah Dare-deVille and Chloe Caution will do a big drum roll on the biscuit tins to introduce this fantastic book!

TARAAAAAAAAAAAAAAAbang bang bangetty-bang (oh well, you can imagine it).

Read on – (and write me a postcard if I've left anything out).

A

ABSEILING

You may think I'm nuttyasafruitcake putting this first as it is possibly not number one on your list of things you think about. BUT, it is for someone, only in her case it's nightmares. **This friend of mine has been having abseiling nightmares about once a month since hearing we are going to do it on our school trip in Year Six.** And guess what? In her nightmare the rope always breaks and she comes plummeting down a sheer cliff about sixty hundred million metres high, and not only dies but squashes her entire family, who are there, all weeping and wailing and

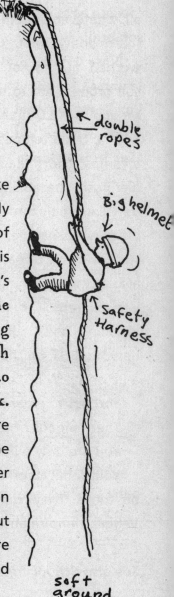

← double ropes

Big helmet →

↑ Safety Harness

soft ground

11

all, whatever, underneath the cliff. These kinds of dream I can do without. Oh, now you think it's me that's worried, but it's not, or not very. All right, I'll tell you if you promise not to tell. It's Chloe, who thinks she is too fat and WOULD squash her family IF she fell on them.

So I, Trixie Tempest Tweenage Tearaway, have found a fantastic formula for Abseiling Anxiety: *don't do it*. (Seriously, there's always a crowd of wimps, um, I mean, Very Extremely intelligent, cautious, or even a little tiny bit nervous people, NOT wimps, who don't do all this stuff and you can always blend in with them.) There is also always a very kind teacher on school trips with a Very Extremely big box of hankies who never goes abseiling herself because she is too wimpy, I mean nervous. BUT, on the other hand, you can always give it a go and it WILL be safe for the following reasons:

You get to wear hard hats.

There's loads of people checking the equipment.

You are only a little bit off the ground.

Your family won't be squashed because they will not be there. They will be at home watching *Vera the Veggie Vampire* and eating choccies and such like.

See also School Trips

ADVERTISING

Put Plumpy Pootch in your shopping bag
Plumpy Pootch for tails that wag!

This little telly ad (I'm sure you've heard it, you know; it's that one where the little puppies are all looking very sad and lonely in a snowstorm and then a big bowl of Plumpy Pootch arrives and the little puppies wag their tails like windmills and then turn somersaults) made me nag Mum to get Plumpy Pootch for our puppies. (Yes! We have five! You can read about them in PETS.) BUT, they turned up their noses at it. In fact, they were all very waggy-tail until it arrived and when they saw it they looked very sad, like only puppies can look, and their little tails went all down and droopy and their ears went all flat, so it had the opposite effect really. They are like their mother and only eat Fidoburgers which is just as well really, as although Fidoburgers are disgustrously expensive, they are cheaper than De Luxe Plumpy Pootch as my mum was quick to point out.

Mum and Dad are always nagging me and Tomato (that's my baby brother, by the way, he's four and built like a tank) not to believe everything we see on the telly. I am beginning to think they may be right after the Plumpy Pootch experience.

But I have discovered that advertising has used all kinds of tricks to make us believe life is meaningless without some important Stuff or other, *for ages*. Way back two hundred years ago, men in top hats were always getting people to believe they had the Secret of the Universe in a bottle. Nowadays, they say they can make life so wonderful that you will feel you have lived to the full, thanks to Gluggo Drain Cleaner or Fairy Barbie, and all, whatever.

Ads also use characters you get used to so they work on you like a Soap. I was upset to discover that Captain Birdseye is not a real person, which horrid old Grey Griselda (my archenemy at school) told me only last year, and also that there never was a Mr Kipling. So he never made those exceedingly good cakes at all. Not even a zillion years ago.

Advertisers defend their porky pies by saying it makes people buy more and therefore creates jobs and all this. But grown-ups are always telling children not to tell porkies. UNFAIR!

AFTER SCHOOL

Help. It's that horrible after school time when you are forced to go to KIDZFUNKLUB and enjoy yourself making dollies out of pasta. Why is this? Because your poor parents are slaving away trying to buy enough pasta for you to eat.

Trixie Tip: Save any spare pasta at the KIDZ FUNKLUB and take a few pieces home with you. Then you can say in a tragic and mournful voice, "Here you are, dearest Mum, I have brought this pasta home so you don't have to work so hard and can PICK ME UP FROM SCHOOL ONCE IN A BLUE MOON." This will make your poor mother cry. Heh! Heh!

More Trixie Tips for avoiding KIDZFUNKLUB: Gettalife. This means, organise tea as often as possible with your best mates. You can have them back to yours on weekends and drive your poor parents mad.

Or, get involved in other clubs you like better. Maybe Drama, or Art or the sorts of things grown-ups think will improve you like ballet – urgh, please, I would rather sit in a bath of slugs (sorry if you like ballet, it takes all sorts and you are very welcome to read this book and send me a rude letter) – or chess if you are brainy or tennis if you are sporty.

If these all cost money then you are going to have to make the best of the KIDZFUNKLUB. Ways of doing this include trying to turn it into a disco or making sure you have your Very Best Favourite book or game with you. Then you can more or less pretend you are at home. I go to KIDZFUNKLUB three times a week (but I don't go in the holidays because my mum is a teacher so she has holidays off, hee-haw) and I have just started doing this and it's made all the difference. I would not like to go home to an empty house, even though I can work the keys and boil an egg and all, whatever. I don't very much like the house's language when it's empty.

ALIENS

I believe in aliens. Obviously. There is infinity out there, so there must be other planets with life on in all that space.

What worries me is whether there are any aliens here on Earth, disguised as humans, like our supply teacher Warty-Beak, to name but one. He has quite a lot of the normal-ish things that humans have and obviously, if he was still in his own alien body, Ms Hedake our head teacher would not have hired him (I think). But his eyesight is like a laser ray, his voice is like a cement mixer (he has an alien translator) and he does not know what a joke is. You know how jokes in different countries are different? Imagine what jokes on different planets would be like. He quite often cackles to himself, so probably that is because he finds pencils incredibly funny or something. Maybe watching someone sharpen a pencil on his planet is like watching someone sliding on a banana skin here.

Grown-ups will quite often comfort you if you have Alien Worries, like will they come in a spaceship at night and do disgustrous experiments on you? Grown-ups will tell you: "Oh, there's no reason to suppose aliens are nasty, dear. I expect they might be very kind. Why should they be any worse than us?" This is the fairy dance idea grown-ups have, that if they say something nice the child will just go happily to sleep thinking, "Ooh. Lovely. If Aliens do come, they will be soft and cuddly and read bedtime stories. That's OK then." Sure thing. And suppose NOT. Eh? Anyway, if they were not much worse than some grown-ups they could be Very Extremely horrible. Imagine the worst grown-up you know and then add tentacles.

See also Zombies

ALPHABET

If you don't know this by now, you should go to the Special Needs teacher and say this: "I do not know my alphabet." She will then teach it to you.

I learnt it by a song that went:

ab C, def G, hijklM,

nopQ, rstU, vwxyZ.

I always hated that song, because it made Z rhyme with M. I bet you did that one, too. But my little brother, Tomato, is doing one that goes different and ends:

See how happy we can be,

Now we've learnt our ABC.

How stupid is that? Why should children be *happy* because they've learnt the alphabet? I mean they can be happy about almost anything, like making mud pies, having a water fight, eating iced buns in front of *Vera*

the Veggie Vampire and all, whatever. But, I ask you. Learning the ABC?

Trixie Tip: Do YOU still muddle up your 'bs' and 'ds'? (If you don't, skip this, but don't laugh, lots of kids do.) If so, use the word 'bed' You can draw it like this:

Then you can remember, easy peasy, because a bed written like this:

would look all wrong.

Last year I made an alphabet chart for Tomato. It was a horror chart. A for AGONY, B for BLOOD, C for CROCODILES. He liked it until W then he got so scared by my excellent drawing of a WEREWOLF that I had to throw the lot in the bin. "Werewolf in bin!

A agony   B blood   C crocodile

D devil   E earthquake   F fear

G ghost   H hound (of the Baskervilles)   I illness

J jellyfish   K killer whale   L Lamia

M monster   N nukes   O ogre

Take way hobble werewolf!" he wailed for days until the bin men came. But I can still remember it and I think I will publish it one day to frighten little kids. Heh! Heh! (Z was ZOMBIE, by the way.) I know, maybe I'll draw the whole thing for you here.

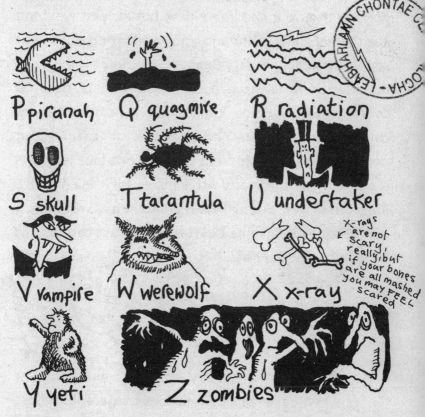

P piranah   Q quagmire   R radiation

S skull   T tarantula   U undertaker

V vampire   W werewolf   X x-ray

x-rays are not scary, really, but if your bones are all mashed you may FEEL scared

Y yeti   Z zombies

Bet you've never heard of a Lamia before – it's a snake with a woman's head. It sucks blood and eats Entrails! Heh, Heh.

ANIMALS

Animals are my favourite thing. I would like to have loads more pets. But this bit is not about pets, you'll have to go to P for that. I don't like the way humans treat our animals so I am a vegetarian. (I don't like the way we treat our children either, but at least we don't eat them, I think, although I am wondering about our supply teacher, Warty-Beak. I wouldn't be at all surprised if he is from a children-eating planet.) Of course, there is nice kind organic farming where chickens and farmers and everyone all roam about pecking freely, but chickens that are not labelled free-range are kept in nasty little boxes for their WHOLE life. These are called battery chickens, which is a sad thing as if they had batteries at least they might be able to move about.

You can try and get your mum or whoever to buy nice free-range eggs whose mothers are having a nice life and also free-range meats where the animals have had a nice life. BUT it is more expensive, so it is a Problem. I'm sure if we all did it, though, it would get cheaper (or cheeper). Or you could be like me and gorillas, and eat just veggies. I KNOW some people think plants have feelings too, but I think that's a bit nuts. Maybe nuts have feelings too? I won't think about that.

Trixie's Burning Question: What do you do when you find a sick bird all sad and lonely in the middle of the road, because it has fallen out of its nest or whatever?

Answer: Well, it could peck you, so if there is a grown-up around, get them to pick it up, so it can peck them instead. Then put it somewhere warm and ring the RSPB (which is like the RSPCA, except for birds).

I think if we are kind to animals, they will be kind to us. As I have never so far been eaten by a lion, that proves my point. *See also Pets*

ART

Art is what you used to do lots of in Infants and where your mum had to be proud to get another egg carton disguised with wool and stuff and try to guess what it was. Sadly, you don't get Art much any more in the Juniors. This is because of a thing called The National Curriculum which thinks Maths and Science and English are Very Extremely important and that Art is something for your spare time.

Art is also what you go and look at in museums and galleries, which are Very Extremely boring places where you are supposed to be quiet. They sometimes try and make this fun for children by having art treasure trails, like: can you find the little furry animal hiding in the Mona Lisa? or whatever. But there are no prizes and lots of rooms to wade through before you can get to the café. **(See also School Trips)**

I am going to put in a little poem here which was written by a girl in Year Six last year. I think it is a good poem because it gives a different point of view from mine and so it may be YOUR point of view.

I Hate ART

I hate art.
I'm supposed to like it, everybody else does
but I hate art.
You get paint in your hair and glue on your dress,
Whatever you're using it ends up a mess.
I hate art.
You've got to make prints with potatoes and wood.
You've got to be 'creative' but I'm no good.
I hate art.
We have to do collages using pasta and string
And tissue and rubbish and any old thing.
I hate art.
And Sarah's horse looks like a horse and
Sam's cat like a cat
But when I drew an elephant it looked just like a rat.
I hate art.
And Emma can draw faces and Rashid
can draw flowers
But mine looks like a scribble even when I've worked
for hours.
I hate art.

And Raoul can mix colours and you should see
Mathadi paint
But when people look at my stuff, they run or
scream or faint.
I hate art.
And I tried and tried so very hard to do something
with clay
But when I showed my vase to teacher she politely
looked away.
I hate art.
So today I just painted a big black square
And under it I wrote 'despair'.
And guess what? It's hanging in the main hall
And teacher says it's the best of all!
I love art.

Me, though, I love art and
would quite like to be an
artist so I could paint and
make pots and stuff all day
and not have to work for
a living.

DESPAIR

B

BABIES

Nia's mum had a baby last month. Poor old Nia. Everyone keeps saying, "Ohhh, your dad's been sexing your mum!" Well, eventually poor old Nia bursts into gallons and floods of tears and THAT is because her dad left home about six years ago and so someone else has been sexing her mum! And I don't think she knows who... Anyway, the head teacher Ms Hedake came into our class and said we were all being very unkind to poor Nia and could we all perhaps make a little welcome card for the baby, to make up. Meanwhile, Warty-Beak stood blushing in the corner. He is not very good at talking about things like that and it is at times like this I wish we had our real proper teacher, nice kind Miss Took. We never realised how lucky we were then, as compared to our supply teacher

Warty-Beak, Miss Took is Heaven in a Basket. She is unfortunately off sick with a very highly infectious teacher's plague. Come back, Miss Took, all is forgiven. I'm sorry I put itching powder in your jumper. I'm sorry if it gave you the plague.

Anyway, I got to make the card! I hope you like it, and we all signed it, even Sumil and Dennis. Nia looked happy and now the baby comes to visit quite a lot and all of us girls go, "coo coo look at is ickle feet," and all, whatever, he is a bit sweet.

I can remember Very Extremely well when Tomato was born, because I was quite grown up at six years old and everyone said how lucky I was to have a baby brother. It was good in some ways, because no one in my class then said anything about sexing and stuff, and I got quite a lot of presents including a real witchy broomstick from Grandma Tempest (but I *can't* make it fly, even though I have read the whole Quidditch rule book THREE times). But I am going off the point of babies. They may LOOK sweet, and if you are a girl you are supposed to pick them up and be nice to them, but I must admit from *first hand experience* that they are Very Extremely smelly and noisy and drooly and I would not want to have responsibility of one myself. Still, maybe when I am an old lady of twenty I will.

BEDROOMS

Here is a picture of my dream bedroom:

Ooh, wouldn't it be LUVERLY

Everlasting Tree →

Clothes-sorter (picks everything off floor and puts away)

Milkshake dispenser

Marshmallow machine

↑ amazing teeny collapsible eight-foot screen, mini-disc, & sound system including 5,000 dvds + 10,000 cds.

Magic → Horse grows full size when you want a ride

Here is what my room really looks like:

The REALITY

BEDTIME (How to avoid it)

You are not a baby any more although your parents still like to think so. They will try all the usual tricks if they are nice (warm milk, a cuddle, even a story if you are lucky, or a story tape) but they will not listen to these four little words:

I AM NOT TIRED.

This is because parents, who seem to be fond of you at least some of the time, really can't wait to get you out of their hair and tucked up safely. They have forgotten what it was like to be ten years old and hear the warm sunshine of the evening street calling, "Skateboard! Football! Fun!" or the delumptious blaring of the TV yelling, "Exciting programmes! Violence! Thrills! Post-watershed Naughty Stuff!"

You can try some of these wheezes to put off bedtime:

1) Sore throat.

2) Tummy ache.

3) Fear of dark.

4) Fear of sleep.

5) Fear of pillows.

6) Say bad dreams wake you up the minute you nod off unless someone sits with you for two hours.

7) Sneak downstairs and if caught say you were sleep-walking.

8) Tell your folks this is the only time you get to chat with them as they are so busy (this will get them guilty), then burble on until *they* fall asleep first. Hey presto: the house is your playground!

9) Yawn a lot. Keep it up from about 6.30 p.m. Yawning is catching, so pretty soon your folks will nod off and you can ask all your friends round for an all-night party.

10) Put all the clocks back one hour (unless your parents have already cheated by putting them forward one hour. Always keep a watch under your mattress so you can be sure of the right time). If your parents HAVE cheated, do one of the the following:

a) Say: How could you lie to me? How can there be trust between us now?

or

b) Put the clocks back two hours.

Write to me and say if any of these work for you.

BED-WETTING

In Year Three I had a friend called Milly. I stayed the night with Milly twice but she never wanted to stay the night with me. One day I asked her why and she started crying. And then she said it was because she wet the bed. Well, I have changed her name to protect the innocent, but I was shocked as I hadn't read Jacqueline Wilson books then and I didn't wet the bed ever after about five years old. BUT I asked my mum about it and she said, "Loads of kids wet the bed and they all think they are the only one and worry about it," and she has spent years of her life telling their mums it's quite normal and common and everyone grows out of it one day. If you are really bothered by it, you can go to the doctor just to check everything is working all right and they can also give you alarm clock thingys that wake you up when you need a wee and apparently get you out of the habit, which is what Milly did. Some people go on pooing as well, and this is more upsetting for them. But it is not a crime and can usually be sorted out by a good doctor or someone nice to talk to, like Mrs Cluck and Mrs Soothe, the two incredibly cuddly Reception teachers in our school. There is usually at least one nice listening teacher at a school and if your school doesn't have even one, then demand to leave as it is obviously a disgustrous place unfit for human consumption.

BEE STINGS

Do not pretend you are not scared of bees. Everyone is scared of bees except little Olaf. Dad's friend Olaf keeps a hive in his garden and I will not go there. But little Olaf, his son, who is twelve, is one of those people who talks to bees, like the horse whisperer and all, whatever, and he walks around covered in bees! I am not kidding! I have seen the photo! (I have also seen a photo of a man wearing underpants made of real live bees. It was called a bee-kini. I bet he had something on underneath it though.) You see, as Grandma Clump would say, it takes all sorts. Best thing for a bee sting, says Olaf, who has never been stung in his life, is TLC. No, stupid, not TCP (which is also quite good) but TLC, that is, Tender Loving Care. Actually, in my own Very Extremely humble opinion, TLC is good for most hurting things. An ice cube wrapped in a FLANNEL is also good, and so is antihistamine cream for when it really gets itchy scratchy. Stings hurt, but they are not scary or dangerous. UNLESS you are allergic or have been stung in the mouth. In that case ask an adult to get you medical help immediately. If you are just stung on your lip, an onion helps. I know it sounds mad, but I have tried it. You have to peel the onion first and then put a sliver on your lip, so it's a bit tricksy and I wouldn't go to the trouble of having an onion in your pocket just in case.

Meanwhile, say goodbye to sting and bite worries!!

See also Wasps

BIKES

At St Aubergine's Primary we have cycling proficiency tests in Year Six and Chloe is miserable about these, even though they are a whole year away, as she has never got on a bike. She tried my bike once and got all shaky and couldn't put her leg over the crossbar. I hope the teacher will excuse her from cycling proficiency tests. I mean, clearly, she is never going to be a cyclist, so she doesn't need them, does she? They are a good thing for the rest of us though. I am rather good on a bike (not to boast or anything) and can do wheelies and cycle along planks with my eyes closed and stuff. I am campaigning for a new bike though as I haven't had one since I was five. It is a problem with being knee high to a pea, you never grow out of anything properly, or if you do, no one notices. My bike, in fact, is falling apart, as it is a Very Extremely rubbishy one we got at a school fair. I will make my parents feel Very Extremely guilty about my bike next year when I have to do the cycling proficiency test and the bike doesn't get its MOT or whatever it is that bikes need to be safe on the roads. Anyway, if you haven't done your test yet, you should not cycle on roads and when you have, you must

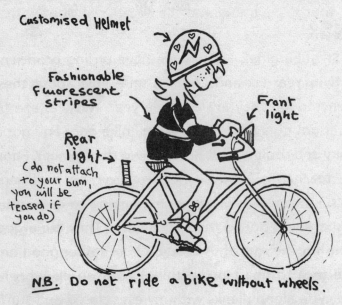

Customised Helmet

Fashionable Fluorescent stripes

Front light

Rear light → (do not attach to your bum, you will be teased if you do)

N.B. Do not ride a bike without wheels.

wear fluorescent stripes all over you and crash helmets and have proper lights and such. I know you don't get cool-looking boys being seen dead in all this stuff, except without it you are more likely to be seen dead. I'd rather look stupid than dead.

BIRTHDAY PARTIES

You know that sinking feeling you get when you find out everyone in your class is going to a birthday party except you? It usually happens like this. You ask your friend to come back to tea. She blushes and says she can't. You ask your next best friend. Same thing. You ask your D list friend and she comes right out with it: "No way! I'm going to Fi-Fi's disco party," she simpers. "Aren't you?" she adds, with a spiteful gleam in her glistening eye.

"Oh, that old party," you say. "Of course. Yeh. See you there," and you go home and cry.

If this has never happened to you then you are either disgustrously popular or you are lying.

One way to try to get invitations to other people's parties is to have really big ones yourself. Depending what type you are (and how much money your parents will spend) you can choose one of the following for your own party:

Ghosty Party Set up camp outside if poss with only a pumpkin for light. Be sure to tell really scary stories. Food should be brains (spaghetti), entrails (jelly) and eyeballs (grapes).

Disco party No point in trying this at home. You've got to spend money, get a DJ (not somebody's dad) and good lights and stuff.

Pirate Party Just take over the local pool. Make sure it has wave machine, slides and boats. Get a real crocodile if poss, to add danger.

This should get rid of unwanted party guests →

A Nice Quiet Party at home with home-made cakes and all, whatever.

Keep Snacks Tasty

None of this healthy grown-up food like raisins and bits of carrot. Go for Pink cakes, jelly, fizzy drinks. Everyone will go manic, which will be fun. The cake must be humungous and full of chocolate, marshmallows, strawberries and smarties. It should have your name on very big, (preferably on every slice) so everyone remembers it was you who gave them such a good time.

Big Fat Party Bags

Excellent water pistols, tattoo transfers, magic tricks, bracelets and sweeties galore.

Photos

Get your mum to take a picture of everyone holding up a big banner saying 'I had fun at Trixie's Party' (oh, put your own name here, if you must). Then they will treasure it forever.

If all the above sounds a bit desperate and like you are trying to buy friends, what the hell. You ARE desperate, aren't you? And better a bought friend than no friend at all. And of course, if you ask loads of 'friends' (bought or otherwise) they will all bring you a present. YES!

Trixie's Burning Question: What's a free gift? Aren't all gifts free?

BOREDOM

'There's no such thing as bored,' says Grandma Clump. Eh?

Matter of fact, I agree, except at school. I am never bored out of school, but in school a weird foggy thing descends on the brain of Tempest, soothing it into a strange, nodding zone where sleep beckons....zzzzzzz. The only cure for this *is* sleep. But when your head bangs the desk and Warty-Beak approaches waving his bony finger and grunting you know it's time to stop.

Cures

1) Paint realistic looking eyes on your eyelids – use your mum's eye make-up or face paint ONLY.

2) Prop head up with Trixie's patent classroom prop (only £6.99 from all good shops).

3) Wire up automatic voice recorder with following

statements to go off at two-minute intervals:

a) "Why, that's a very interesting fact you told us, Mr Wartover."

b) "Goodness, the capital city of the USA is Washington, not New York, you silly billy."

c) "Stop talking, Sumil, I'm trying to listen to Mr Wartover."

Your recordings can be custom made to suit any lesson and wheeeeee, off to the Land of Nod!

NB: You can use these tips for any occasion that bores you. For homework, you just paint the eyes on and glue a pencil in your hand and you can sleep quite a while as your parent will just peep round the door and tiptoe away, thrilled you are studying.

Excellent painted-on eyes

Pencil taped to finger

BRACES
See Dentist

BULLIES

"Sticks and stones may break my bones but words can never hurt me."

Hands up who thinks that is true?

I bet NONE of you put your hands up!

That is another of those grown-ups' fibs. How is it that grown-ups so quickly forget the golden days of childhood?

Being called fatty, spotty, thick, smelly and all, whatever, can hurt as much as being given a black eye. It can feel worse, because you can show everyone a black eye and get sympathy.

Bullies always pick on someone they think is smaller, or weaker, or more frightened than them. This is because they are often small, weak and scared themselves, so picking on someone is the only way they have of feeling big and strong. The bullies at my school are Orange Orson, who pushes my head down the loo to try and get my lunch money, also Grey Griselda and her gang. Grey Griselda is the worst kind of bully because she doesn't *look like one*. She has flowery dresses and plaits with pink ribbons and fairies on her lunchbox and she simpers at the teachers and does annoying things like helping them wipe the board and put out chairs, but all the time she is giving you a Chinese burn or an 'I'll see you later in the Quiet Corner' look.

Grown-ups say, "Be calm in the face of a bully." They say the bully will get bored of bullying you if you do not look upset. Grown-ups tell you to say, "No. Go away, I do not like what you are doing to me." Ooooh, I can just see those grown-ups saying that to Hitler, or whoever. What is the point? Is the bully supposed to say, "Oh. Sorry. I thought you liked me holding your head down the loo and cussing your mum."

But if you say, in a very firm and Very Extremely confident way: "If you don't stop NOW, I will tell my parents and they will tell the head teacher and the head teacher will tell your parents," that *can* work. If you are being bullied and it is making you ill or scared to come to school, definitely the best thing is to tell someone you really trust. Your parents/carers or teachers should protect you and they can only do that if they know what is going on. Some people are ashamed of being bullied, as though it means they are a weed or something. But that's NOT TRUE.

It is a really good idea to hang out with your pals as much as possible, so that a bully can't get you on your own – and if there is no one at school you get on with, or you find it Very Extremely hard to make friends, then make sure you always look as though you are doing something important, like taking a message to a teacher, or fetching the football for someone else, or reading a very important book on how to get a free sweety supply for life, or something even cooler like learning Chinese. That will fox them. Also, learn a martial art! Martial arts classes teach you to protect yourself by *avoiding* fights, and only fighting if you really really have to. It is no good getting into fights with bullies; it is cool just to say, "I don't need to fight you and I don't want to fight you." But it can be good to demonstrate that you could make mincemeat of them with your super-judo-karate-kung-fu techniques if they were worth the time and trouble, instead of being the sad worms that they are.

There are some primary schools that have a special law court for bullies. There are two kids and two teachers on the judging panel, and if the bully is guilty, he or she gets to write lines or stay in or do something boring or useful or both. And bullying in these schools has gone down! 'Cos the bully feels stupid! Mmmmmm. I am going to start one of these bully courts at St Aubergine's. Speaking out against bullies and getting help is not telling tales; it is brave.

We had a brilliant talk at school from someone from Kidscape, an organisation that's dedicated to keeping kids safe. Check out their website on www.kidscape.org.uk. And don't forget, you can call ChildLine free on 0800 1111 – DON'T BE SCARED TO ASK FOR HELP.

BUM

This is Tomato's favourite word. Once you are in Juniors you find this word less funny than you did, as I keep reminding Tomato when he runs through the kitchen going, "bum bum bummety bum" in front of my friends. Mum says, "Trix, you must learn to ignore the unwanted behaviour and then he will stop it." Hmmph – just because she's a teacher. How can I ignore a little red cannonball with a very LOUD voice?

Talking of teachers, a teacher's bum should, if possible, be encouraged to sit on a whoopee cushion at every opportunity. However, don't try this with Warty-Beak, if he ever comes to your school. Or with your head teacher. They might not appreciate it and you might have to stay in during playtime.

See also Teachers, Rude Noises

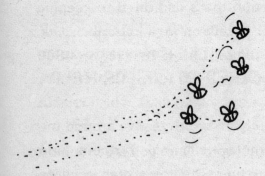

C

CARTOONS

It is Very Extremely important to allow kids to watch cartoons as much as possible. Cartoons help exercise the laughter muscles of the solar plexus, which release important fun loving zygotes which prance around the child's body and promote wellbeing! Cartoons help brain growth and digestion. They also keep children fitter than book reading because of interesting eye movements owing to the speed of the pictures.

This research has been done by Very Extremely important science people.

(Now that the above is printed in a real book, you can photocopy it, cut it out and paste it on your parents' wall.)

See also TV

47

CATS

You are either a dog-person or a cat-person. Doggy people are friendly and fun and open and chatty. They wriggle when you talk to them and that is because they are trying to wag their tail, which they used to have a long time ago just after dinosaurs. Catty people are mysterious and cool, with paws. They are descended, I think, from lizards. I am a dog-person. I like the way dogs are always pleased about everything. Here is a dog's day:

7.00 a.m.

Whooppeee. Humans coming downstairs! Doncha just love 'em! Lick lick licketty-lick.

7.30 a.m.

Breakfast! The best!

8.30 a.m.

Yes! Out for a wee wee. Fantastic! Wag wag Waggety wag.

8.45 a.m.

Postman! Yeah!

9.00 a.m.

Hurrah! A drink of lovely water! Wag wag slurp.

10.00 a.m.

A little roll! And a nap! Lovely!

11 a.m.

A little play with my ball! Oh fantabulous!

And so it goes on all day. Until:

5.00 p.m.

Family home! Fantastic! Who do I love most? All of them! Wag wag wag lick lick lick bounce bounce bounce.

6.00 p.m.

Hey! Lucky me! I'm going for a walk! Oh joy!

7.00 p.m.

Food! Too much happiness!

7.30 p.m.

Another walk, oh wow!

8.00 p.m.

Dad home. Yes! Great!

And so on.

Whereas here is a cat's day:

blank

or might be think-ing of little dead bird.

7.00 a.m.

Stretch. Yawn. Drink, eat, look bored, nap.

Midday

Chase some innocent mouse or birdy. Eat it if possible. Lick lips.

7.00 p.m.

Stretch. Yawn. Drink, eat, look bored, nap.

I think I have made my case. But you must make your own minds up!

Trixie's Burning Question: Has anyone made budgie flavoured cat food?

CEREAL PACKETS

These are a cheat. They never have the cards that you are collecting or else they advertise some 'super fun' toy that any fool can see is a cardboard circle with a picture on it. Who do they think we are? The few with really good stuff are the ones your mum won't buy.

See also Advertising, Crazes

CLOTHES

Keep it simple. Three pairs of jeans. Six T-shirts. Six tops. Fancy skirt.

If you're a girl, make sure jeans have flowers, sequins, stars and stuff like that. Boys do not care about clothes. They have one top, usually, although their mothers will force them to put it in the wash every fortnight and then they will turn up in their big brother's top or occasionally their sister's, which will make them sad. Sumil came in last week in a pink fluffy cardigan, but being Sumil, everyone thought it was cool. That's because Sumil is naughty. If he was good, people would have teased him.

Disco crop-tops and belly studs go down badly with teachers but are Very Extremely popular with other girls. Most Tweenage Tearaways, if asked: "Would you rather be loved by teachers or other girls?" might not say "Teachers", of course, but being sent home for trying to look like Christina Aguilera can be a drag.

Kids who have all the latest designery stuff can still look like buffoons, so if your folks can't afford or can't be bothered to get you fashion items, either make your own or just wear your old rubbish with confidence! I don't have any posh shoes. If I wear a skirt, I wear my pink trainers with it and socks with rainbow stripes. It suits me.

COUNSELLING

If you are unhappy, there is usually someone at school who will put you in touch with someone who you can talk to. They can find out about lots of things that may have caused your unhappiness (i.e. nasty teacher when you were five, nasty parents all the time, no potty training, too much potty training, too few sweeties and all, whatever), so then I suppose you can at least feel you are unhappy for a good reason.

Happy people sometimes go to counsellors too, just for some little problem, and then they realise how many Very Extremely Big Problems they could be suffering from without realising it. They soon become Very Extremely unhappy.

See also Bullies, Violence

CRAZES

You are in the playground, keen for a game of footy or 'It' and everyone else is standing around feeding electronic pets or swapping *Pokeynose* cards. And you don't have any *Pokeynose* cards. So you beg your mum for *Pokeynose* cards or you get the cereal packets with *Pokeynose* cards in and you are baffled and flummoxed (I hope you like that word, it means you have not got the faintest idea what is going on). And you find that to understand *Pokeynose,* you have got to know about fifteen different countries (none of them real) and eighty zillion different teams and four thousand and seventy kinds of martial art moves and you find you have traded a mega card worth about a squillion maxi cards for one measly mini card and you have done this to be in with the in crowd. They are all laughing their heads off at you and rolling around waving their legs in the air because you are the one fool who doesn't seem to have understood this craze AT ALL. You lie awake in bed wondering how everyone knew about this stuff before you did. How do they know that a Bandyfluff is worth ten Zoonlumps and can disarm a Flugbot with a mere flap of its tentacle, whereas the mighty looking Mothworm needs to get sixteen bungs to be able to vanquish Lord Snoop? "Help," you say.

But look, if you have Craze Worry, then don't hang about moaning that you don't understand it, or make a fool of yourself by trying to, just start your own!

You can use some of the names I've made up, or make up your own. Or you can start a craze about something everyone's heard of. I started a James Bond craze last year and everyone went around for a whole year saying, "No, Mr Bond, I expect you to die." It was a shame Dennis said it to Warty-Beak, but apart from that it was cool.

Or you can start your own secret language. This is a craze everyone wants to do. Here's my secret language. You can use it with your BF but don't tell ANYONE ELSE, OK?

Step one: You take the first letter off each word and add it to the end, with a 'y' following. So 'Trixie' becomes 'rixiety'.

Nothing new there, I hear you say.

Step two: But then, you add dibbly to the first word of the sentence, dobbly to the second and docus to the third. So 'Trixie likes marshmallows' becomes 'rixietydibbly ikeslydobbly arshmallowsmydocus'.

Sounds hard, but after about four months' practice, you and your BF can become really quick.

Other people HATE it when you can do this and they haven't got the slightest idea what you're on about.

CROSSING THE ROAD

This is scary the first time you do it on your own. Trixie Tempest's advice? Just hold someone's hand. It gives you confidence. Look all around loads of times and only go when you know it's safe. Don't run after your mates, think for yourself.

D

DARK

If you have never been scared of the dark you can skip this bit. Usually, things that go bump in the night do not seem to go bump in the day and if you have any little niggling worries they will often, by about 11 p.m. have become Very Extremely enormous, gigantic, slobbery, jelly-like terrors, waving their tentacles about and moaning. I do not know why the dark does this, because if you think about it, dark is just a thing that happens in between days as a result of the sun going round the other side of the world.

Whoops, I mean, the world going round the sun, well you probably know that as you probably did the solar system in Year Three. This is an encouraging thought, as when it's night time in England you can always think of it being day time in Australia. You can think of all the Aussie people jumping around surfing, and all, whatever, which is quite cosy. Grandma Clump used to try to cheer herself up by thinking of all the little cats' eyes on the road twinkling away all night. It is just as well no one told her that they were only lit up by cars' headlights and were not, in fact, twinkling all by themselves.

I like to think of parties and discos all loud and cheery. This might work for you.

Trixie's Night Time Tips

If you have a carer or babysitter who tells you scary stories at bedtime, ask them not to. If they go on, hum very loudly. If that doesn't work, snore loudly and pretend to be asleep. They will then think – aha, thank goodness I can now go downstairs and watch TV and stuff crisps and all, whatever.

If a parent or big brother or sister or anyone else scares you about big bad monsters coming to get you if you don't go to sleep IMMEDIATELY, tell them you don't believe a word, or scream very loudly indeed until they stop. I heard a horrid story once of a girl who NEVER crept into her parents' room, because she had been told there was a giant on her ceiling and he would eat her if she got out of bed!

Avoid scary videos at bedtime unless you have already seen them a zillion times and know what to expect. (Even *Vera the Veggie Vampire* has given me nightmares, so it is quite hard to judge what will make you scared.)

Keep a torch and your favourite book handy by your bed.

Go to sleep with a tape on.

Keep your door open so you can hear cheery sounds from the rest of the house. They won't keep you awake, but they will be comforting.

If awake, think cheery thoughts as above.

As a last resort, go into parents' room and scream!

See also Sleepovers

DENTIST

Grandma Clump says dentists used to yank your toothypegs out with pliers and string before they got skilled and started using road drills that sounded like Hell's Angels' motorbikes. Now it's all quite quiet and painless, so I'm told. But I haven't had a filling yet. It may be that tooth cleaning is a Big Thing in my family or it may be I'm just lucky. I eat enough sweets...

Dinah's mum is trying to make her wear a brace. WHY? Dinah is NOT goofy. Apparently, when your teeth or jaws don't line up properly it is called 'malocclusion' and the dentist may recommend braces to make it better. Now that you know this wonderful word 'malocclusion' maybe you can surprise your parent or dentist (if your parent IS a dentist you can surprise them both at once) by saying, "I am quite happy with my malocclusion thanks very much and I do not want sticky old braces that get sprouts caught in them." Some braces are fixed and some you can take out (choose the second if you HAVE to have them) and they slowly force your toothypegs back into shape. This gives you a nicer smile, apparently, though I would think that would depend more on your general face.

If you have to have braces you have to be Very Extremely careful about tooth cleaning and all this as the braces collect food (OK, not sprouts, you probably never eat sprouts, but any stuff) and that can lead to holes and the dreaded drill! Also, avoid sweets (great) and even avoid crunchy stuff like apples and carrots. So that would be rubbish if you were a horse. As far as I know, animals do not have braces. Get back to nature and STAND UP FOR YOUR RIGHTS.

DIVORCE

Sometimes, when I am having a little, or Very Extremely big worry, I wonder, what would it be like if MY parents got divorced? Where would I go? Who would I choose not to be with and would that hurt their feelings? Then of course I remember that my parents aren't married at all! So they CAN'T get divorced! Then I feel cheery. But THEN I think, WHY aren't they married? So you can't win, really.

I hope Dad isn't going to gallop off into the sunset but if he did, I would gallop off after him on Merlin and lasso his new wife and say,

"How can you steal this loving dad from his little girl and even littler boy? You heartless hussy!"

(Hussy is a rude word for a Bad Woman that Grandma

Clump uses about just about everyone on the telly and everyone wearing a skirt shorter than Victorian times. She is a bit old-fashioned sometimes but she makes a mean apple dumpling. In my class lots of kids are from single parent families but I don't know whether many of them had divorces or what. They don't seem any different to me, but their single mums and dads do look a bit tired. I would not like to bring up Tomato without a bit of help, I must say.

I think it is really UNFAIR that kids feel bad about their parents divorcing and think it is their fault as they asked for too many sweeties or whatever. This is not true.

If your parents are getting a divorce and it is making you sad and worried about who you are going to live with and how often you are going to see the other one, try to talk to them about it. You could also talk to your favourite teacher and ask if there is a counsellor you could speak to.

See also Counselling

DOGS

My favourite animals after horses. Dogs are so nice and loving and yummy. Here is a drawing of some typical doggy types (with their dogs).

Choose the one who suits you best. (As you can see, dogs often look exactly like their owners. Or maybe the other way round.)

See also Cats and Pets

DRACULA

See Dreams (and Nightmares), Vampires, Zombies

DRAMA

I have only ever had one speech in a school play. It was:

> *Come birds and bees*
> *Come from your trees.*
> *Come bees and birds*
> *And hear these words.*

I practised it every day for weeks but when the day of the performance came, my mouth got very dry and this is what I said: *nothing.* I went on saying nothing for what seemed like six hours until Ms Mortice, our deputy head teacher, said, "Come birds," to remind me. Then I said: "Come birds and words and trees and bees." All I remember next is quite a lot of laughing.

We did Aladdin as a Year Four Christmas show last year and I am very sorry to say that I did not play Aladdin, or the Genie, or Mrs Wishy Washy. I had to play a bit of treasure in Aladdin's cave. I had a suit made out of cooking foil – Dad said I looked like a sparrow done up for the oven. All the little bits of treasure had to dance about singing a twinkly song. I enjoyed this about as much as sitting in a bath of slugs, but it did give me an Idea. Maybe *I* could make a lamp that would grant MY every wish! I kidded Chloe that this would work with Tomato's Thomas the Tank Engine night-light, and when she wished – as I knew she would – for a lifetime's supply of marshmallows, I pulled a string which brought a whole pillowcase of them down on her head. Sadly, she went on believing it was real for days, and I had to keep thinking of excuses for why we couldn't use it again until finally I had to  confess the Awful Truth. This experience convinced me that I could be a very good actor – or liar – I am not sure what the difference is, but none of my teachers has yet seen my great potential. Dinah, of course, who can do anyone's voice, will one day be a Big Star, and I will remain unnoticed and go on playing the mouse pulling Cinderella's coach, never, sadly, to be Centre Stage. Still, I can play the trumpet, which is a lot easier.

DREAMS (AND NIGHTMARES)

Dreams are two kinds: daydreams like becoming First Child President of the World (which I will do when I am twelve), captain of England football team, Olympic horse riding champ and so on. These are Very Extremely good for you and cheer you up all the time. **Child Experts say that children need lots of time for daydreaming and it is cruel to interrupt them** (paste this on your teacher's wall). There should be at least five daydreaming lessons at school every week where we can just gaze out of the window and imagine ice-cream mountains and all, whatever.

Night time dreams are more tricky as you don't have any control over them. Very long ones can happen in the twinkling of an eyelid – they seem to last forever but in fact are only a second long.

I think when dreams are v. nice they cheer you up, but when they are horrible they are a Very Extremely pain in the butt.

When me, Dinah and Chloe talk about our dreams, we all seem to have dreams about falling or being chased – so they must be very common. Also dreams about doing something really horrid that you would never dream of doing in real life. Those can be Very

Extremely scary. I once dreamt there was a vampire in Bottomley and it appeared at midnight and drank people's blood. In the dream, I was reading about it, with Dad, in the paper. And we were both saying how scary it was. And THEN the clock started striking twelve and I realised I WAS the vampire!

I started running up a scary winding staircase, because I didn't want Dad to see me change into the vampire. It was horrible. Of course I woke up before the clock got to midnight. I can tell you that was WORSE than dreaming about being chased by a vampire. I thought it meant I was a Bad person when I woke up, but Mum said it doesn't. All these things are just your sleeping mind trying to make sense of a whole lot of stuff that's been going on in your life.

If you have the same bad dream again and again, it is a good idea to imagine the dream had a good ending.

But Bad Dreams are just part of life and dreaming is Very Extremely good for you.

See also Sleepovers, Dark

E

EARS

This should be sung to the tune of: *Do your ears hang low?*

Do your ears stick out?
Can you waggle them about?
Are they bigger than Dumbo's?
Do they make you want to shout?
Do people say they'd work for flying?
Which makes you feel like dying.
Do your ears, stick, OUT?

Lots of kids have sticky-out ears but here's the Good News. Not many grown-ups do. That's 'cos your face kind of catches up with your ears eventually and although your lugs may look like bat's wings just now they will seem to shrink and flatten as your face gets bigger. Oh well, that's what my mum says and maybe she's right. Or maybe we're the first generation of kids with all sticky-out ears because we've had too many fizzy drinks or something and the human race is in fact turning into aeroplanes as a part of evolution. Great. We'll be able to fly then.

Do your ears have wax?
Does it come in lumpy stacks?
Does it worry you at all?
Do you want to know the facts?
Do you think your wax is grotty?
Do you feel it drives you potty?
Do your ears, have, wax?

Listen, everyone on the planet has earwax. It's sometimes yellow, sometimes dark brown, and Very Extremely useful as it has little chemical thingies in it that kill germs, also it keeps dust off your eardrum. So there. If it gets very thick so you're having trouble hearing, the doc can soften it with oily ear drops. But never try poking it out yourself. You will only poke it IN, and could damage your lugs.

Do your ears have rings?
Are they dinky little things?
Did you get them pierced?
Can you tell me if it stings?
Is your earring like a gem?
Oooh, I'd like one of them.
Do your ears, have, rings?

My mum says I can't have my ears pierced till I'm twelve. So pooey to all you lucky nine, ten and eleven-year-olds-who've had it done already. I hope you get ear infections, NOT! But if your mum says you can have your ears pierced, make sure you go to someone good who sterilises all the stuff and measures your ear lobe properly. I know this sounds daft, but if you have thick lobes (no offence) they might use a thingy that's too short and then you will be uncomfortable as the whole thing will be too tight. My mum has told me all this to put me off, I'm sure. But don't use nickel – use stainless steel or 14 carat gold. You can see I've found out a lot about this because I am Very Extremely desperate to get mine done. You can't get any nice earrings with clips any more. Only baby ones made of plastic. That's enough about ears.

EMERGENCIES

If you have a *real* emergency – frinstance someone is badly hurt, you've seen a crime committed, you are lost or badly frightened – and there is no adult to help, you will need to phone 999. It is FREE. PC Toecap came to school and told us how to make an emergency call so now I can tell you. You dial 999 and someone will answer and ask you for your phone number – this is in case you get cut off – and which service you want: Police, Fire or Ambulance. You then get put through to the right service, and someone else will ask you for your phone number and where you are. They will then come out and find you and deal with the emergency.

Never be one of those stupid kids (I name NO names) who dials 999 for fun. You will be haunted by the thought that some little old lady was being mugged and no one went to save her because you were 'taking up valuable police time'.

See also Stranger Danger

ENVIRONMENT

Did you know a whole acre of rainforest is disappearing every second? That's bigger than St Aubergine's playground. Rainforest is where parrots live, apart from being useful in other ways of course, and I think it is disgustrous that we are shaving it off as though it was some old beard we didn't like.

Grown-ups like to tell us what to do but it seems to me they are not making a very excellent job of things and it is up to us kids to help them sort it out.

Such as:

Recycling. You can persuade your school to have recycling thingies for paper and you can persuade your mum to do bottles and paper and cardboard and all sorts of stuff. If your area doesn't have recycling you can write to the Council and ask WHY NOT?

Ask your teacher why they don't have a recycling thingy for paper.

(Er, don't recycle loo paper though.)

Don't keep nagging for lifts to school either. It is better for you and the air if you walk!

Don't leave taps running while you clean your snappers.

Share the bath water (that means using it first and letting your brother in after you – on NO account do it the other way round in case your little brother pees in the bath).

Trixie's Burning Question: What should you do if you see an animal from an endangered species eating a plant from an endangered species? Answers on a postcard please...

EXAMS

Next year, when I am in Year Six, I will be forced to do the Horrible Dreaded SATs exams to show that I can add up, write a story and know what 'essential life processes' are. As far as I am concerned, the essential life processes are: laughing, running about and chatting, but I do not feel the examiners will agree with me. We had to do some tests when we were seven and they were pretty stupid: they gave you little bits of stories and you had to say whether Mr Mole lived in a nest or a hole and all, whatever.

But the ones next year are worse, because you have just forty-five minutes to write a story. JK Rowling takes three years to write a new Harry Potter adventure! OK, so maybe her story is 600 pages and your story is one page. It has still taken her (hang on, I will get my calculator out) 2,920 hours (that's eight hours a day for one year) multiplied by three, which equals 8,760 hours to write 600 pages. So, um, divide 8,760 by 600. And you get 14.6 hours! For each page! So it takes a fully grown famous author more than fourteen times as long to write a page than it is supposed to take an eleven-year-old. Pooey to that.

Also, these exams make all the school so Very Extremely boring. You do less Art and Music (and my mum is a teacher and she says Music is especially good for every kind of learning – not that I care, but Music is my favourite thing so I'm sure she is right) and you don't bother to read whole books, just stupid little bits of books which you have to practise being tested on. And everyone gets all hot and bothered and worried – teachers, kids and parents who worry their little cherubs are not getting high enough marks. Bring back childhood! STAND UP FOR YOUR RIGHTS!!

F

FARTS
See Rude Noises

FEAR
Here are some of the things I have been scared of:

staying in the bath with the plug out:
I used to be convinced I would go
down the drain with the water. I am
still not 200% sure this might not
happen in someone else's house,
where maybe they have a
bigger drain.

Falling down the loo: The result of falling into the loo is being eaten by a crocodile. This happens regularly in the USA where they have crocodiles in the sewers. But now I am a grown-up girl of ten, I can see that the U-bend is too small for even me to go down. I do still hold on to the seat, though. I wonder if anyone else does, but it's not a question you can ask people really, until you know them quite well. "Hello, pleased to meet you. Do you hold on to the loo seat?"

Spiders: I used to scream when they sang *Incy Wincy Spider* at playgroup. I thought the water spout was like any old tap and I didn't want spiders coming out of the bath taps. Combine that with the plug hole fear above and you can see why I was scared of having baths. About 75% of the girls in my class have Spider fear. It is called ARACHNOPHOBIA, so that is the excuse you can use.

"Sandra, why are you never in school?"

"I am arachnophobic, Mrs Web, and must wait till I have a teacher with a new name." And so on.

But look, you can be scared of anything if you really try. You could try PANTOPHOBIA, not a fear of big woolly knickers, but a fear of Everything! Or even PHOBOPHOBIA which is being scared of being scared! Hey, now you've thought of those two, I bet you don't feel scared any more.

Trixie Tip: If you are scared of a teacher, imagine them in long red woolly underpants. Try not to giggle.

FOOD:

If I had marshmallows every day I would be 'happy-as-larry'. That's what Grandma Clump says and I agree. I like also caramel ice cream with chewy bits. Cheesy strings, marshmallows and tomato ketchup is what me and dear old Cautious Chloe have for a midnight feast. Daring Dinah's mum would NOT allow that.

I HATE: liquorice, marzipan, coffee. Ugh! Why do grown-ups drink that stuff in gallons? Our usual teacher, Miss Took, always has two cups on the go. She says she needs a cup every five minutes to stop her shouting at us. It's true, it works for the few seconds the cup is actually attached to her lips, but after that the volume goes right UP. Maybe she's off sick because of caffeine poisoning. Well, I wish she would come back so that we don't have to have Warty-Beak, the horrible supply teacher, instead.

My mum is Very Extremely keen on *healthy* food.

Five fruits and veggies a day frinstance. Well, five baked beans is fine by me. But it's breakfast cereal that drives me kerazzy. My fave is Krispy Popsickles (Hear them Popsicrackle! Hear them Popsipop! Once you start Popsickling, you'll never stop!) but Tomato always eats them first and I get the Organic Muesli, or Shredded Beets, or Sand Puffs. Which would YOU rather have; organic green flakes and bits of bogey that look and taste like pocket fluff, or some cheery Krispy Popsickles? Or, better still, Chocolate-covered charmy Hoops, which I think have now been banned for having lovely marshmallows in them, but which bob about all pretty colours in Tomato's Thomas the Tank Engine bowl looking like sweeties while I sit with my tongue hanging out. And anyway, that bowl used to be MINE. I MISS that bowl.

Never use one spoon when you can use two

But Trixie Tempest has just recently done a survey of the ingredients on the side of the packets. And guess what? There is hardly any difference between Organic Fruity Crunch Muesli and outrageous Krispy Popsickles!

In fact, Krispy Popsickles have got ADDED vitamins and minerals. So there!

Tell your mum, tell your dad. Shout it to the world. STAND UP FOR YOUR RIGHTS!

I still can't eat a shiny red apple, just in case some mirror somewhere is saying 'I'm the Fairest of them All' and some wicked old step-mother is sharpening her knife. The most excellent fruit is banana. It comes in its own wrapping and everything. Neat AND sweet.

Anyway, be sure and eat from each of Trixie Tempest's Essential Food Groups each day:

Chocolate.

Potato.

Marshmallow.

Banana.

Peel & cook, then mash with loads of butter

Oh, all right then, since this has got to be published and teachers will stop you reading it unless I put in something GREEN, you can add green Smarties (but the orange ones are nicer).

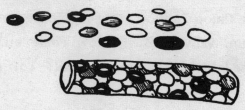

FOOTBALL

The best game in the Universe. And I know. Because I have seventeen generations of witchy blood running through my veins, and I can therefore time-travel to other planets in my sleep, I can guarantee that there is no game like it. There is a similar game on Zepx, except the people there have eight legs, so it is quite complicated and they play with four balls.

Actually, I am not supposed to tell about this time-travel trick of mine because people will think I am mad, so promise not to tell anyone, especially my dad.

There are some girls, quite a lot actually, who do not understand the beauty of football and unfortunately my BFs, Chloe Caution and Dinah Dare-deVille are two of them. Why is this? How come only boys are supposed to kick a ball around? You do not have to be a rocket scientist to do this, or even particularly strong. You just have to have legs. Try it.

NB: Teachers do not encourage girls enough. I bet the time will come when we will be just as good as boys. Remember, once there were no women doing anything at all! They just used to sit around sighing all day. We have come a long way since then. And we will go further. Right to the very top of the Premier league.

FRIENDS

It is Very Extremely sad when the friends you would LIKE to have do not seem to want to have YOU.

It does not usually mean they don't like you, it probably means that they have not noticed you. If, even though you have done cartwheels and painted your face like a rainbow and all, whatever, the friend-of-your-dreams just walks past, you will just have to look somewhere else. I know I am Very Extremely lucky to have TWO very good friends who are *at my school.* But that is only because I have known them since we were all in playgroup, so we all feel cosy with each other. Even though Chloe can be really annoyingly Cautious and Dinah can be really annoyingly Noisy and

Over Confident and I expect they may find me really annoyingly something or other, but I'd rather not think about that just now, so I won't.

I think the reason we have stayed BFs is because we stand up for each other. All you really have to do to stay BFs, I think, is be nice to each other. And most of the time we are. I think grown-ups see kids as very simple creatures, who have a very simple view of the world. THEY think we see each other as either 'cool' or 'weird'. But kids are smarter than this. We know we're cool some of the time, and weird some of the time. Everyone is a bit of both.

Look at Chloe. She wears lumpy jumpers and wouldn't say boo to a goose and goes bright red like a little fat luminous postbox if she gets told off. In fact, the teachers have all learnt not to tell her off, because she looks so sad. Even if someone says "No," very nicely to Chloe, it will have the luminous postbox effect. BUT Chloe always has loads of sweeties on her, she can draw and she is just so NICE. She is ridiculously nice. She knows what it is to be hurt and so she wouldn't hurt a fly. She's weird AND cool at the same time.

Now Dinah. You would think Dinah, who is a brilliant mimic and can do everyone's voice that you ever heard of and is going to be an actress, would be a super cool person. But she can be very weird, too. She talks to herself, frinstance, and often makes a weird humming sound that she isn't even aware of, like a bee with a sore buzz. Also, she is scared of heights. I mean it, she can't even stand on a chair.

If you really are feeling left out and lonely, try to sit next to a kid who you think is really popular. See if you can do some stuff with them, even if it's photocopying for the teacher. Look around to see who you like the look of, and find out what things they like. Then see if you can do it with them. Get your folks to invite them somewhere exciting, and all, whatever. This will help, especially if it is somewhere you know they are dying to go. It also helps if David Beckham is your dad; you can probably get any friend you like then.

But in the end, if you just Be Your Self – as Grandma Clump would say – other kids will respect you more than if you try too hard to fit in. Everybody's different from everyone else. But we're all also quite alike. And one of the things we nearly all want is to BE liked. So take a lesson from Chloe. Be nice. If you're nice and friendly and kind, people will find it hard not to like you. Honest.

G

GENIUS

If you are feeling at a loose end and everyone else is into a craze that you can't stand, it is a Very Extremely good wheeze to take a term or so posing as a genius. All you have to do is read a book in Egyptian hieroglyphics. There is a very good chance that no one

'i' & 'e' are the same and Trixie is a bit dull, but if your name

begins with A or H or L you are in luck with hieroglyphics

in your class will understand these. You could try Latin, unless you are in one of those posh schools where everyone is learning it already. Or you could study the nose flute. Or wear a Genius hat (squashed top hats or very old berets will do) and scribble poetry in the Quiet Corner of the playground. Make sure no one ever gets near enough to read it, but murmur that your publisher needs to keep it quiet until your book is published. People will then think of you as a nutty professor type and gaze at you with new respect. Maybe.

GOALS
See Football

H

HAIR

My hair is a mat. It is a quite nice yellowish colour, sort of dark straw. It isn't like 'blonde'. Blonde is all rippling waves of satiny pale gold like an angel's halo. No. Mine is like what you line the rabbit hutch with. Also, it's really coarse. Like a horse's mane. I usually put it in bunches to keep it out of my eyes

although I did do it up in beads for World Save the Bead Day, but often I just let it hang about my face. It looks like a haystack even if I put on Shimmerkins conditioner and SLEEP in it. Someone told me you can get smooth hair by sleeping in olive oil. I mean, putting olive oil on your wig all night, not actually sleeping in a bath of the stuff. That would be dangerous, of course. You are supposed to wash it off next day, but I was late for school and forgot. It is quite odd going to school with hair covered in olive oil, you should try it. You will be very glad of your normal haystack afterwards.

We had a hair growing race at school in Year Four. We all measured our wigs, then took bets (unfortunately in boring old *Pokeynose* cards) to see whose hair grew quickest after a month. Guess who won? Dennis, whose head is usually shaved like a billiard ball. He looked like a mad professor after just one month. Haddock-face Hannah cheated (oh, maybe I haven't mentioned her before, she is quite nice but she does look exactly like a fish). She measured her hair in inches the

Dennis

before →

after →

Haddock-face Hannah

See? Same length. CHEAT!

first time and used centimetres the second! Cheapskate.

I never thought about my hair until about a year ago. It was just a cuddly mat to keep my nut warm that annoying grown-ups made me break a comb on now and then. But recently I have found myself sneaking looks at models and pop stars and feeling envy. Am I growing up? Anyway, Trixie Tempest says: If you don't like your hair, join the Hair Haters club. You are no different from anyone else.

Nobody wants the hair they've got. Grown-ups are even worse than us kids in this respect. You see those old ladies leafing through the leaflets at the hairdresser and saying "that one please," at some swanky blonde with, like, pleated hair. But what they are really wanting is the face.

Learn to love your hair, it's there to keep your nut warm.

HEADLICE

If you are the kind of person who has never had a nit, then you had probably better stop reading this and stay home cosy in the world of the nit free, reading nice stories about pixies and ballet dancers. In my school, nits jump happily from head to head like they are doing a special little nit song and dance routine:

We're not here to make you pretty,
We're not here to make you witty,
We're here to make you scratch your head,
Until you wish that you were dead.
This is the nitty ditty.

"Ooooh! There's Trixie again," they squeak in their tiny nit squeaks. "We haven't visited old Trixie for a whole week. If we jump on her now we can hitch a ride on her brother again and spread all through nursery school."

(Unfortunately I have got nits at the moment, but don't worry, *you* can't catch them from reading a book.) But now, my little brother Tomato's got nits too. And Mum's got nits. And I've got really rather a Very Extremely big lot of them, a whole housing estate of nits is settled on my nut, complete with nit camper vans, old nit mattresses and all, whatever.

Warty-Beak told us he had nits a long time ago. Well, it must have been sometime last century, because

Warty-Beak does not have enough wig to support even the poorest household of nits. He has two strands of hair pasted down over his lizardy forehead. Any self-respectin' nit offered Warty-Beak's nut would go straight to the Office of Fair Housing or whatever and ask for a rent rebate.

"Nits are nothing to be ashamed about," creaked Warty-Beak, baring his crocodile fangs as we all nittered, I mean, tittered. "The proper name for nits is *Pediculus Humanus Capitis*. That is Latin," he continued, "a wonderful old language used by the ancient Romans and sadly no longer 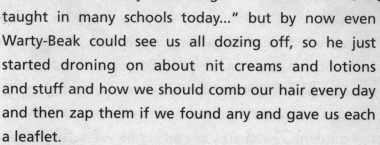 taught in many schools today..." but by now even Warty-Beak could see us all dozing off, so he just started droning on about nit creams and lotions and stuff and how we should comb our hair every day and then zap them if we found any and gave us each a leaflet.

I put some nits under Dad's clever pen thing that's a telescope one way round and a microscope the other. They look yellowish and transparent, and they have surprisingly cuddly fat little legs, like tiny sausages. I've tried to explain this to Mum but she always stops me and complains of feeling suddenly ill.

HICCUPS

Sorry, but too much fizzy drink usually causes these. If they go on for three hours, go to the doc. Otherwise, get a friend to press just in front of your ears (on the bony bit) on both sides while you SLOWLY drink a glass of water. It really does work. Other things, like pouring a glass of water on the sufferer or, better still, dropping the glass of water on a tiled floor with a horrible crash and scarifying bits of glass shooting off in all directions, are more fun and might work too.

HOME

Here is a picture of my perfect home.

In it, there is always a parent making marshmallows or pancakes with golden syrup. There is a ping pong room, a pool room, a tennis court. There is a horse in the garden. The chairs are as big as sofas. The sofas are as big as beds. The beds are the size of swimming pools. The swimming pool is the size of the ocean. The ocean is just outside the back garden anyway and has a beach of silver sand. There are no schools for miles around so you have to be taught for about an hour a week by a kindly tutor with pockets full of marshmallows, who teaches you about marvels and mysteries and magic.

Just one wing of Tempest Towers

HOME ALONE

You shouldn't be left alone at home at ten years old, so you'll just have to go to KIDZFUNKLUB. (*See After School*) But if you *have* to be left at home on your own, ask yourself these questions:

Do you feel OK about being on your own?

Can you follow simple rules responsibly? i.e. "Do not play with matches."

Can you find things to do without getting into trouble? i.e. Now is not the time to experiment with your big brother's chemistry set labelled '*Nuclear devices: Only to be used under adult supervision*'.

Can you deal with unexpected situations? i.e. Tornadoes.

Can you get in touch with your folks easily, on a mobile, frinstance?

Is there a neighbour around in case of emergency?

Have you worked out what you would do to get rid of someone who was trying to get in? I would dig a moat round the house and have a big boxing glove on a spring just inside the door and a big pot of treacle balanced above the door.

AND REMEMBER, if you are alone at home, don't answer the door to anyone, unless you were expecting them – for eggsample, Chloe and Dinah would not be too happy if I didn't let them in.

It's good to get some practice in being at home alone, as one day you will have to be. You'll then have to do boring grown-up things like making sure the door is double locked and feeding the dog ALL BY YOURSELF. Practise by letting your mum, dad or whoever walk round the block for two minutes, so you get the feel of the house. Extend this to ten minutes, and so on. If you don't like being alone, TELL THEM. You will not be a wimp for doing this.

HOMEWORK

Here is a little item from St Aubergine's Parents' Handbook.

Homework helps your child to grow into a responsible grown-up. She or he will learn to keep promises, meet deadlines and be successful in the workplace. Responsible children finish homework on time.

HUH!

I think homework does the opposite of the above. You do it really badly to get it over with, so it encourages sloppiness (as Warty-Beak would say). It encourages dishonesty, as in forging notes from parents to say you were sick, or pretending it got dropped down the loo by your brother. I have done this twice and am now wondering whether saying it got blown away in a hurricane or eaten by the dog would convince Warty-Beak.

I think it's disgustrous making us do so much homework. We have it twice a WEEK. Some kids have it every DAY! Grown-ups don't go to work all day and then bring homework home! And grown-ups are paid to work! (Oh, all right, I bet you say that to your folks and they say they're always working and you don't know you're born and all this, but that's even more reason not to do the same thing to kids, isn't it? I mean to say, this is the only childhood we've got.) And look, why will it do me any good to colour in a map? I can colour. I'm not learning. I would quite like to know where the map is of, and what the towns are and all this, but usually it is a silly map with just one town and not even an ocean named.

HORSES

If you know what an Appaloosa is, you are probably mad keen on horses like me. (Oh, OK, just in case

you're on *Who Wants to be a Millionaire* one day and this is the million pound question, I'll tell you. An Appaloosa is a spotted horse, like a Dalmatian.) But to me, all horses are beautiful, from little cuddly Shetlands to great noble carthorses, they are the most beautiful animals on earth. Not only is a horse as gorgeous as a lion, but it lets you ride it! Imagine if you could ride a lion! But sorry, this is not Narnia, and you can't. I had ten riding lessons last year as a birthday present from my witchy grandmother. ("You might as well do something useful, since you can't make the broomstick work," she wrote.) I discovered then that riding makes you feel strong and free and wild – a bit like skateboarding but better because you have this friend (the horse) who is doing everything with you – and ever since I have been saving every penny to buy Merlin, my Dream Pet, the palomino that only lets me ride him, gallops like the wind, has a cowboy saddle and so on and so on. I am not sure whether he will be Horse of the Year or Derby winner, but he will probably be both and I will be the most Famous Child President Horse Riding Champion ever. Dinah's parents have billions of money and they have said they will buy her a pony if she is still mad keen when she is twelve – and she goes riding every single week. She is soooooo lucky. But she says she will let me ride her pony! I have got to keep her keen on ponies and keep her away from boys, which I have noticed often become more interesting than ponies when you get to be about twelve. I find that very hard to imagine, myself.

INVISIBLE FRIEND

When I was four, I had an invisible friend called Bert. He did a lot of stuff with me, but he was Very Extremely naughty and I got the blame.

Bert did the following:

Broke the kitchen window.

Broke the bathroom window (twice).

Broke the neighbour's window (three times – he was a terror with a football).

Put Dad's electric drill in the washing machine on fast-coloureds heavy soil.

Made an adventure playground in the street with a lot of my dad's old planks. It was Very Extremely good, but PC Toecap came round complaining that cars needed to use the road sometimes, which is typical of grown-ups.

Bert did lots of other silly stuff like putting salt in the

sugar bowl and washing-up liquid in the squash bottle and silly dangerous stuff like that which I would never do.

Bert was always persuading me to join in his plans but no one ever believed me and I always got the blame. So when I was six, I said, "Bert, I have got to be sensible now and so have you."

And I never saw him again.

My mum says, "He wasn't an invisible friend, he was an imaginary friend." But I'm not so sure. Maybe I will run into Bert one day in prison or somewhere.

INVISIBLE INK

No home should be without invisible ink. Sadly, some are, but many of these thoughtless homes will have a lemon, which works just as well. Just write your message in lemon juice. In order to read the message, the reader must warm it with a candle. You have to light the candle first, so of course a responsible grown-up must be present or within screaming distance.

Trixie's Burning Question: How do you tell when you've run out of invisible ink?

j

JELLYFISH

I did a thing about jellyfish for an animal project in Year Four. Everyone else chose kittens and puppies and little cuddly things, except me and Sumil. We did jellyfish, and it was the best. In fact, I think the jellyfish project was the only thing of mine that ever got on the classroom wall. One day my teachers will probably cry when they read this and think: "So that's where we went wrong. We never encouraged poor little Trixie and that is why she is in prison now."

Anyway, here are some things me and Sumil discovered:

Jellyfish are found in ALL the world's oceans. They have no HEART!

They have no BRAIN! They have no BLOOD! Their food is called ZOOPLANKTON! (this is made of lots of other little fish including other jellyfish, so they are CANNIBALS! They trap these poor little fishies with their TENTACLES! They swim using JET PROPULSION! Their stings are little HARPOONS! They can just be a mild rash or they can KILL YOU! The most dangerous jellyfish is the Australian box jellyfish which is more poisonous than a COBRA! So there. Who needs aliens when you have these little critters sailing about under your very nose.

If you should meet a jellyfish while swimming, be sure to have a paper plate and a party hat with you. It might think you are celebrating and that you are intending to have jelly for tea. With any luck it will scarper. In fact, some people DO eat jellyfish, so good luck to them.

However, even Sumil and me had to admit in the interests of nature, science and love of animal life, that there is an up side even to the disgustrously villainous jellyfish: most of them are harmless to people, they provide shelter for tiny crabs (aaaaaaah) and some are being used to treat illnesses. Isn't nature wonderful?

K

KEYS

Er, don't put your name on your keys. Make sure your mum or dad or whoever looks after you has given spare ones to a nice neighbour in case you get locked out. Keys are not suitable for swapping, even if your BF has the nice flowery pattern one that you can get now. Her keys won't work in your door. I bet you knew that.

Does your key ring reveal much about your personality? Er, no.

Ɫ

LEFT-HANDED

"All the girls on Dad's side of the family are left-handed," says Grandma Tempest. She thinks it is a sign of being a witch. In fact, I use both my hands (left hand for writing and drawing, right hand for everything else). So I am ambidextrous and therefore Very Exceptionally clever or Very Extremely stupid, depending on what stories you believe. Back in ancient times when Grandma Tempest was a girl, left-handed children (though not witches, of course) were forced to use their right hand and grew up mad and stuttering. Now people are kinder, but lefties can have problems with scissors and stuff and end up with a reputation for being slow and clumsy. Teachers like Warty-Beak never seem to offer you different scissors and pens and all, whatever, they just pretend not to notice that you are struggling. If you're having problems cutting things out or whatever, tell your teacher.

For writing I always have the paper turned sideways and write from top to bottom. I like to sit on the left of any desk so I don't bash elbows with whoever is next to me.

STAND UP FOR YOUR LEFTS!

PS: Did you know that The Queen, Bart Simpson, Julia Roberts and Paul McCartney are all left-handed? And so was Lewis Carroll, who wrote Alice in Wonderland. So there.

LOOS

Grandma Clump says when she was a girl they only had horrible scratchy loo paper everywhere. In public toilets it was stamped with the words 'Government Property'. And nearby there was usually a sign saying 'Government Property must not be soiled'(!) She thinks the best invention ever is soft loo paper. Me too (after marshmallows). Especially after too many marshmallows. So WHY do schools insist on having this disgustrous old ancient medieval loo paper? Join Trixie Tempest's campaign for proper loo roll in schools! Nobody I know ever does a number two in school. I suppose this saves the government a lot of money because none of this scratchy stuff that is like putting sandpaper on your behind is being used at all and they need fewer loo cleaners. But school loos are disgustrous in all ways; they don't flush, they have big gaps under the doors so big girls can look over the door at you on the loo and little girls can squash under to have a better look. You can never get to use them at St Aubergine's without a toilet card! This is criminal. **Down with school loos! STAND UP FOR YOUR RIGHTS!**

LOSING STUFF

There is a poltergeist at home who takes our stuff. Mum says, "I put my glasses down here on this table just now ONE second ago. And now they have vanished." Dad says, "I put my hammer in the sink (I know this sounds odd, but this is the sort of thing he does) ONE minute ago and now it has gone." This happens every day, but not just to the grown-ups. I used to think it was Tomato taking the stuff, but it happens to him too, mainly with socks or Heffalump, which is his favourite cuddly toy (a rhino, since you ask). Heffalump always disappears at bedtime so I thought he was hiding Heffalump to put off going to bed, but no. He cries and cries and wails and wails until we find Heffalump each night, which often takes an hour. He also never has his socks. I never have my socks either and Dad never has his. I blame my mum for this as she is not a Very Extremely good housekeeper in

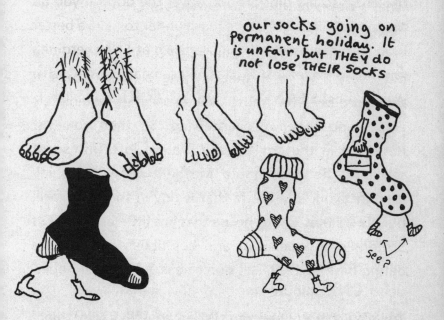

our socks going on permanent holiday. It is unfair, but THEY do not lose THEIR SOCKS

see?

my humble opinion. In fact if she was as scatty about marking homework as she is about running her home then she would get the sack.

I told Warty-Beak yesterday about the poltergeist. I said it was always taking things and that it had just taken five socks, one set of house keys, my dad's cheque book, so he couldn't pay the milkman (although I think that might have been Dad telling a porky) and my homework. As a result I have had to stay in at playtime today and write I must not lie to my teacher. Oh, what a clever teacher I have. What interesting lines he makes us write.

My mum has now introduced a 'lost things' box. You put everything in it that is lying around where it shouldn't be. The house will quickly be completely empty and the box overflowing. So then you just rummage in the box for stuff you've lost, instead of searching the whole house. Maybe it will work. I think it might work in a house that is tidy in the first place, but ours is that sort of house that has little bowls full of buttons and paper clips and bus tickets and pennies dating back to 1972, so I don't hold out a lot of hope.

Trixie's Burning Question: When you find something, why do grown-ups always say, "It's always in the last place you look?" Are there people who go on looking *after* they've found something?

LOSING YOURSELF

This is more scary than losing socks (see above). You can lose yourself in a beautiful dream, of course, though you are likely to be brought back to reality by a screaming Warty-Beak. Or you can lose yourself somewhere else in which case you need to have a mobile (huh) or get to a public phone and ring your mum or dad. Or you can go into a shop and ask them to phone for you, or ask a police officer to help you. **BE SURE** to wait till someone you know comes to pick you up. Never let a stranger drive or walk you home.

M

MANNERS

Parents and teachers are always telling you to say sorry. It is a bit rubbish really, because you know your enemy doesn't mean it if they are forced to apologise.

"Orson! How dare you try to push Trixie's head down the toilet! Apologise to her immediately."

"Sorry," scowls Orange Orson, scuffing his trainers on the floor and giving you a look that says see you outside later and if you don't give me all your lunch and your sweety money I will make sure it is not just your head in the loo next time.

But there are *loads* of ways that people say "sorry" as a habit when they don't really mean it. Those big, shambling blokes who look like yaks and push you out of the way to get on the bus sometimes say it (if they notice you're there at all), so do Very Extremely busy looking people with suits and mobile phones who crash into you and say sorry without even noticing that you have hurtled off their elk-skin briefcase into the path of a speeding truck.

I think grown-ups should learn to be more polite to kids, as they are constantly asking US to be polite to them. When did you last get a thank you letter from a grown-up? OK, all you sent them was a handmade card that took you hours, but you haven't got enough money to buy them stuff, so they should say please and thank you, especially teachers, who just shout "how dare you" and "get out" and all this. But if WE shout, we get Lines! Or staying in at playtime! Blah blah blah. Humph.

I would like to have a Talkback Day. We could talkback, only we would be Very Extremely polite and show the grown-ups up!

Here are some examples:

Mum to Toddler: "You must share your sweeties with Samantha."

Toddler: "Please give that nice lady at the next table half your pudding."

see how your mum feels about sharing her pudding..

Teacher to Child: "Do up your laces this minute."

Child to Teacher: "Would you be so kind as to please do up your trousers."

Angry Old Man: "Get off that skateboard, I'm walking here."

Child to Angry Old Man: "Please could you wait a minute, or step off the pavement for a second, as I am not allowed to skateboard in the road."

MATHS

Will somebody please tell me what Maths is for?

All I want is an answer. What is it FOR?

What, what, what is it one, two, three, for?

I can see you need a bit of counting

So you can work out, say, a football team.

I can see you need a bit of adding

So you can work out, say, the price of sweets.

I can see you need a bit of subtracting

So you can work out, say, your change from

the sweet shop.

I can see you need a bit of dividing

So you can work out, say, whether you got your fair share.

I can see you need a bit of multiplying

So you can work out, say, well, I don't know really,

maybe how many more sweets you could have had
IF you had more money.
But otherwise, really,
What is Maths FOR?

And why do we have to know what an octagon is?
Have you ever seen one except in a Maths book?
Can somebody please tell me,
What is an octagon FOR?

At St Aubergine's some of the clever kids are doing a thing called algebra. I had to sit in their class for being naughty and it seemed mad to me, all about As equalling Bs. WHAT is the point? Whoever heard of someone actually using algebra in real life? Frinstance:

"Where's the sweet shop?"

"Well, if the post office equals X and the burger bar equals Y, then the sweet shop will be Z squared."

"Oh, thank you, most helpful."

Please can some teacher who uses very simple words like: "This is what algebra is FOR, I'll show you," write me a letter telling me what algebra is for. Then I can put it in my next book and help thousands of tweenagers the whole world over get happy.

MONEY

I have got to say here that although my mum is a teacher who should know better she often forgets to give me pocket money and then I get embarrassed to ask for it. I don't know if this happens to other kids much, as I am too embarrassed to tell anyone that I often don't get it. How pathetic, I can hear you say, but when Mum and Dad are constantly moaning and complaining about the cost of everything, then it makes me feel bad, asking for stuff.

But I need money Right Now at this moment for the following: Sweets! Comics! Cinema! Jewellery! Transfers! Ear piercing! To impress my friends! I also need it for new football boots, **new trainers (my current ones were a bit mashed by Bonzo, who thought they were an exciting pair of pink Fidoburgers)**, a crop top for the Year Five disco and about a thousand other things. And I cannot raid my Merlin fund else I will never get my Dream Pet. IF you haven't read my other books you won't know what I'm talking about, so go and nag your poor parent to buy those books now (oh, OK then, my Merlin fund is my savings to buy Merlin, a palomino pony who gallops like the wind).

I am always nagging Mum and Dad to do the lottery but they only ever do it once a year! Why? We could be rich with holidays all year round and horses! If I won the lottery I would get millions of horses and enough marshmallows to last my whole life.

Here are Trixie Tempest's tips to make a few quid quick:

Car cleaning is quite fast, although in our street they seem to have cottoned on that the car wash at the garage is slightly cheaper and much better. How unfair is this?

Lawn mowing. Hard work, not recommended.

Windows, ditto.

Front path sweeping.

Dog walking. If you are a dog-person, this is the best although you must do it with a friend or an older brother or sister, in case an evil stranger jumps on you.

But OK, if you have a parent like mine who does not remember your pocket money and when you haven't had it for about two months says vaguely, "Oh yes, sorry, how awful of me, I must owe you three whole weeks." OR, if you have a parent that thinks that 50p will still buy you anything worth having, I think it is fine to say no guilt, time to strike. And go on children's strike. This means, you stop doing anything around the house that is helpful, stop going to school, stop being sweet, stay up all night, insist on watching adult TV. Say, since you are not being respected as a child who deserves pocket money, you have decided to behave like a grown-up.

Otherwise, you can always wheedle for a rise, like this:

"Please can I have one hundred and sixty-eight pounds a week?" (At their look of shock, you say your teachers always tell you to aim high, and so should they, then go on to explain.)

"That is only one pound an hour, which is considerably less than the minimum wage." (This will impress them with your Maths and also your knowledge of current affairs. Quickly continue to stage three.)

"Well, you love me, don't you?" (They will say money has nothing to do with love and that you should never try to buy love. You say that money has a lot to do with happiness and surely they want you to be happy, don't they? With any luck, this won't lead to a discussion about whether money actually does buy happiness, but will make them feel guilty and sad at which point you go in for the kill.)

"OK, I understand, I'll settle for less."

This could raise your pocket money from 50p to a couple of quid if you play your cards right.

MUSIC

Music makes me happy. I have about forty CDs and that is a lot more than most people I know and they are all kinds of things; I like Jazz and Bob Marley and Jurassic Five and Eminem and Girls Aloud and Lemar and Classical so you see I am not just a Top of the Pops person. Love songs make me sad, but most music just makes me want to dance. My biggest thing I love most apart from horses, is my trumpet.

The trumpet is good because you can get to the point where you can play a simple tune and it will sound quite nice in just a few lessons with a bit of luck and a good teacher. My teacher, Danny Vibrato, is really cool. To play the trumpet you have to vibrate your lips over the mouthpiece, a bit like blowing a raspberry and you shouldn't really try it until you've got all your second teeth (although I did, because I still have one annoying baby tooth in front). I would like to play like Miles Davis when I grow up and if you haven't heard him play, you should.

Trixie's Burning Question: If practice makes perfect but nobody's perfect, why practise?

NICKNAMES

Nicknames have a habit of sticking. For example, Stinky isn't something you want to be called for your whole school life, even if it's done all friendly and so on, and only means you set off a stink bomb once.

Mr Wartover is Warty-Beak. Well, if you are a teacher with a very big nose, a lot of warts and a name called Wartover, it is up to you to change one of those three things, isn't it?

Tiny Euripides is Lofty, which is much nicer than his real name. Great big Faroukh is Pee Wee, which is OK. But poor old Ramesh is Rubbish.

Everyone likes Ramesh, but he doesn't like his nickname and you can see why. Quite a lot of people call me Sticks. It might be because my arms and legs are like twiglets but I think it's because it rhymes with Trix. It's OK, anyway.

If you hate your nickname, I don't think there's much you can do about it except "Grin And Bear It" (thank you, Grandma Clump) as if you make a fuss it is bound to stick harder. You could try and get your BF to call you something else and hope it catches on. This did work with Chloe, who was called Hoglet in Year Three (don't ask me why unless it was her mammoth capacity for sweeties). So we worked out a new name for her and me and Dinah called her, as loudly and often as possible, Bunny. And it caught on! And now everyone just knows her as Bunny. Mind you, there are a lot of people who would prefer to be called Hoglet than Bunny, me, for one. But Chloe prefers Bunny so there you go.

NITS
See Headlice

NO OFFENCE
If anyone says to you: "No offence, but..." you can be sure they are going to say something disgustrous. Close your ears and run... fast. Also run if they say: "I think you ought to know..." as this sentence usually ends with "everyone hates you. I'm your friend and I know you'll

thank me for telling you." Also run if they start with: "Not to be rude or nothing, but..." You can be sure this sentence will end with something Very Extremely rude that you do not want to hear. If everyone ran away screaming Very Extremely loudly when anyone said anything like this, there would be no more wars.

NOT BEING LISTENED TO

Being ignored by family, friends, teachers and all, whatever, can be very hard to bear. I get upset even when the postman fails to ask me how Harpo is. But part of a good life plan is learning to take the slings and arrows of ignoring people on the chin. (I don't know why they say "the chin"; the slings and arrows seem to hit me in all parts of me at once.) If this was all our chins had to put up with, life might be a bowl of marshmallows.

Ignoring includes: BF for forgetting your Birthday (If your parents do this, seek adoption); teacher failing to notice you although your hand has been waving pitifully in air for half an hour; mother asking you how you spell your name and all, whatever.

Horrible Ignoring people can be better than Horrible Nosey people though, like well-meaning relatives and so-called friends who kindly say things about how skinny/plump/tired you're looking to your mum when they think you're not listening and your mum replies, "She's always been dwarfish, poor love." Mind you, I did once say Chloe looked a bit plump in those purple shorts she wore at sports day but I think that was just kind advice.

Anyway, horrible ignoringness and horrible noseyness are just part of life, so get real, stop whingeing and realise, in the words of Grandma Clump, that You Are Not The Only Pebble On The Beach!! Boo hoo.

NUTRITION

This is about healthy eating and balanced diets and all, whatever.

It is a way of making food (a Very Extremely nice thing) into a Very Extremely boring thing. I am fed up of tables and diagrams and plans saying what food everyone should eat. So I have made up a child friendly diet sheet. (*See Food*)

O

I cannot think of anything for O so here are some things beginning with O that I like. Please write and ask me to write about them if any of them worry you:

OMELETTES, ORANGES, OWLS.

And here are some things I don't like: OGRES, ONIONS, OYSTERS. I bet you agree.

Lawks – it's an ogre with a giant owl AND an ogreish onion

P

PARENTS

We all have two parents, even if we don't know who they are. Most of us still live with both our parents, although if Grandma Clump is right, there will soon be hardly any two-parent families, as she is certain that everyone will get divorced sooner or later, which is not her usual cheerful view of the world. Grandma Tempest says witches don't care about things like marriage even though she has been married herself for about a hundred years and has sixty-eight grandchildren.

Parents exist to earn money and read bedtime stories. They also provide food (sometimes by cooking it) and clothing, with the exception of matching socks. Added bonuses should be treats, outings, holidays, presents at Christmas and birthday and most weekends, sweeties and comics most days. In return, children should remember to give their parents love and affection, because we are not yet earning enough money to do anything else. Parents like to be treated with consideration and need regular routines to help them feel secure.

A typical car journey routine, frinstance, should include you saying "are we there yet?" every three seconds until your parent bursts into flames. If you are quiet and read a book for the whole journey they will worry and think you are ill. Similarly, if you go shopping and fail to nag them for comics, sweeties, ear piercing, flower tattoos and all, whatever, they will find life strangely quiet and boring and begin to question whether they are Good Parents.

Trixie Tip: Keep 'em keen, treat 'em mean. If you are too good, your parents will not have enough to do and may wish to develop interests OUTSIDE THE HOME. This will be very bad for family life.

PE

This is when you have to wear shorts and climb up ropes and jump over horses. It would be fine if they were real horses but those boring horses they have in school are just old blocks of wood with legs and they are too high for me. And I am sporty! Poor old Chloe, who is not sporty and in fact finds it quite worrying going up steep stairs, always gets a note for PE. And Pee Wee, who is the size of four buses, doesn't go swimming, because he is shy of being called Eight Bellies Pee Wee. There must be a better way... I think PE should be more things, like dancing frinstance, which everyone likes if the music is good. And, of course, football every day.

PETS

Respecting your pet(s) is one thing you can do and as someone with an allergy to dogs who still has one on her bed most nights, I know what I'm talking about. Lots of pets are abandoned every year after Christmas when spoilt brats like me decide that the cute ickle ball of wool is not such fun when it asks for walkies all the time and wees all over their Barbie. Also, it quite quickly turns into a vast panting hound demanding half a cow for breakfast. THINK B4 you get a pet, whether you really want to look after it, rain or shine. If you DO, it will reward you with loads of love and may even inspire you to write a book...

You can read about my dog Harpo in *Trixie and the Amazing Doggy Yap Star.* She is a big wuffly sort of dog and for about two years she has been in love with Lorenzo, the handsome but thoughtless red setter next door and father to Harpo's five puppies! They are the sweetest puppies in the whole wide world, I think, especially Bonzo who I am determined to keep for my very own forever.

You would think that since seventeen generations of witchy blood flows through my veins, that I would be a cat-person. But if you've read C for Cats you will know that in fact I am a dog-person (and particularly at this Very Moment in time right now, a puppy-person). But I do know that cats can very occasionally also be Very Extremely loyal and devoted.

I had a hamster once called Smokey. Unfortunately life got on top of old Smokey and he just didn't wake up one morning. I cried for a whole day. We gave Smokey an excellent good funeral with proper music. Dad put on a long black coat and played the Funeral March on a comb and loo paper. But the Funeral March is a very solemn bit of music and it didn't sound quite right played like that, so first me, and then Tomato got very bad giggles. You know those sort of giggles that you

get when you know you are going to explode. And at old Smokey's funeral too. I got very sad about that later as I thought of poor old Smokey looking down from Hamster Heaven and seeing us all pink and giggly when we were supposed to be thinking only of him. He must have thought we didn't care. But we DID. Bonzo didn't. He dug up poor Smokey's remains the other day.

I also had a Goldfish, Sydney. Sydney was cool. He lasted a good long time for a goldfish, but when he eventually floated quietly up to the top of his globe, we put him in a matchbox for a coffin and floated him down the canal at the bottom of our street, like dead King Arthur going off to see Valhalla. He got stuck on quite a few Special Brew cans and old chip papers (Sydney, not King Arthur, I think it was a bit cleaner back then) but he finally disappeared looking really peaceful.

I wrote this on Sydney's coffin: *Oh, wet pet.*

See also Cats, Dogs, Horses, Nits

PHOBIAS
See Fear

PIRANHAS

I was shocked by how small these little creatures are. If you didn't know about them you might be tempted to take one home in a bowl. They look quite cuddly, but beware, they can strip your flesh in seconds. Why not introduce one to the school nature table?

PLAYGROUND

Please write out this letter and send it to your MP. Add some bits of your own:

Dear...................

There are not enough playing spaces for children in ....

Please can you build a Very Extremely big enormous exciting adventure playground with flying foxes, nets, tightropes and very big climbing frames on ....

This will keep children off the streets. But please pave the streets over too as we kids are fed up of cars.

Thank you.

Yours sincerely,

....

It is rubbish how few decent playgrounds there are in Bottomley. All we have got is a sand pit and four swings and a broken old seesaw and a little train covered in graffiti. I used to love this little train

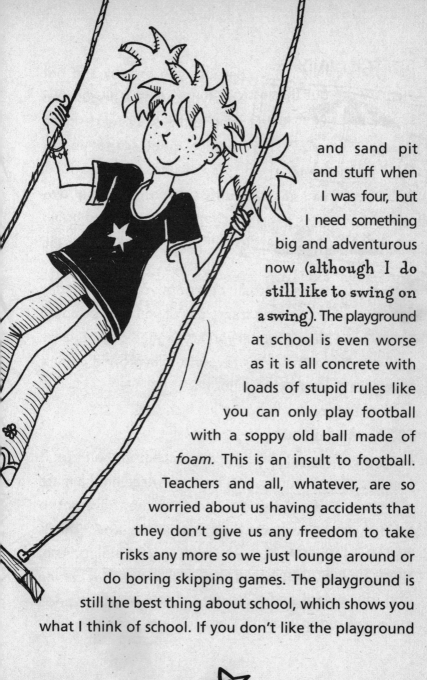

and sand pit and stuff when I was four, but I need something big and adventurous now (although I do still like to swing on a swing). The playground at school is even worse as it is all concrete with loads of stupid rules like you can only play football with a soppy old ball made of *foam*. This is an insult to football. Teachers and all, whatever, are so worried about us having accidents that they don't give us any freedom to take risks any more so we just lounge around or do boring skipping games. The playground is still the best thing about school, which shows you what I think of school. If you don't like the playground

Milk shake
Fountain

because you are shy and not sporty it can be a disgustrous place to be, so I have designed a nice quiet corner in my playground (see beautiful illustration) that allows dreamy types to read books and play poker or all, whatever.

If you don't like football, or it's not your football day or it's not your climbing frame day or you hate skipping or you have played tag till you are tagged out, here are a few of Trixie Tempest's favourite playground games. Introduce them to your school!

Out of the Freezer

Everyone walks around with a beanbag on their nut. If you lose your beanbag, you have to *freeze* until a mate picks it up and replaces it for you. But they have got to keep their beanbag on their nut all the time. This is only really good if you do it hopping, or running. Also, you have to have the kind of school where they can be bothered to give you beanbags, which St Aubergine's hardly ever does.

"Oooh, we don't have enough beanbags for everyone, dear, and some people might get left out and feel sad." Pooey to that. Isn't it better for some people to have fun and a few people to be sad than everyone being sad?

Rottweiler

One person is the Rottweiler. Everyone else lines up at one end of the playground. When the Rottweiler goes, "woof woof grrr," everyone runs to the other side of the playground. Anyone caught helps the Rottweiler until everyone is caught. The last person to be caught is the next Rottweiler.

James Bond Tag

One of you is Goldfinger. Everyone else runs. If you're caught by Goldfinger, you have to say, "Do you expect me to talk?" and Goldfinger has to say, "No Trixie Bond (or Dinah Bond, or Sumil Bond, or whatever your name is) I expect you to DIE." (*See Crazes*) If Goldfinger gets your name wrong you are free. If Goldfinger gets it right, you have to stand still with your feet apart pretending to hold a gun (like the posters of JB) and hum the Bond theme. (Dan, da da dan, dan, dan, dan, repeat.) You can only be freed by someone crawling between your legs and singing the rest of it. (Dan dan, dan dan, da da dah!) This is a good one for the whole school, as Goldfinger can only freeze people if she or he knows their name.

POETRY

In Infants we had a little book that we put a poem in every week and we learnt the poem. We don't do that any more. WHY? Poems are fun. If we didn't do stupid old SATs exams I bet we would have more time for poetry. My favourites are limericks. You know, the ones that go:

There was an young lady called Trixie...

but of course the playground version of these are Very Extremely rude. Perhaps that's why we don't do much poetry in school any more.

POLITICS

If politics was all government and prime ministers, it would be a bit less interesting than cement. But politics is also animal rights and environment and stuff which I am interested in so maybe I'll get interested in the House of Commons and all that one day so I can be First Child President of the World and pave the streets with marshmallows.

Maybe I will join this thingy called the UKYP (I think that stands for United Kingdom Youth Parliament) where children can have big talks on important issues like more playgrounds and less cars and such like. But you can't join it until you're eleven. Unfair. I am going to form a real Kids' Parliament for ages six to twelve (I think five is a bit young as Tomato will NOT be ready in just one year, he doesn't know a jellybean from a Smartie).

POTIONS

I'll let you in on a secret if you promise not to tell. I still like making potions. One of the few Very Extremely good things about having a little brother is that you get to have fun pretending to be younger than you are and playing ghosties and pirates and making potions. Tomato's favourite potion is a mixture of: egg, muesli, washing-up liquid, green food colouring, coffee and earth!

But there are endless combinations, most of which have ended up on the carpet or in Dad's breakfast bowl. Heh! Heh!

I hope it's OK to go on making potions until I'm about fourteen. Maybe I'll have to be a chef, so I can go on stirring with dignity.

PRIVACY

Tweenagers need privacy. Demand locks on all doors, especially the bathroom (ours is always broken and I can't sit on the loo for five seconds without Tomato barging in waving a sting-ray laser gun). Mum and Dad go on and on about their privacy but seem to think my life is their business too! "Who was that on the phone? What did they want? Where are you going? Look at the state of your hair/hands/shoes/clothes/face/room." And all, whatever. If I talked to them like that they would go up the wall.

I think it would be quite good if children sometimes talked back a bit more than we do.

See also Manners

QUESTIONS

What was the best thing before sliced bread?

Why do parents take kids on treats just to shout at them?

Why doesn't superglue stick to the tube?

Why does 'fat chance' mean the same as 'slim chance'?

Would the sea be deeper without the sponges?

If these are the 'best years of our life' why wreck them by giving us homework?

Why do teachers think shouting works?

Why do crumpets always fall butter side down?

Do animals have souls?

Do people have souls?

Do plants have souls?

Do slugs have souls?

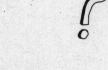

Do parents really love all of their children equally or do they just pretend?

Do plants feel pain?

How do **DO NOT WALK ON THE GRASS** signs get there?

Why are girls told to brush their hair more than boys?

Why don't we just pave the streets with gold instead of keeping it all locked up in banks?

Why can't we eat sweets in school? Grown-ups can eat sweets at work.

How do people who drive snowploughs get to work?

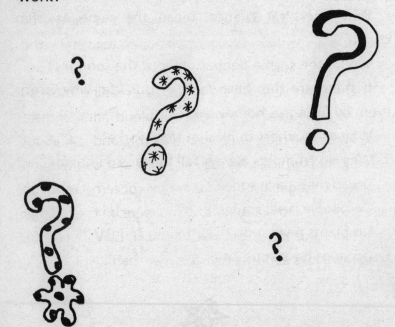

READING

You will find that although your parents hate you doing most nice things (TV, computer games, Playstation, sweet eating, having fun) they LOVE it if you are curled up with a book. Unless you are like Roald Dahl's *Matilda* and LOVE reading so much that you do it most of the time, *then* your parents will probably hate it and say, "Why don't you do something useful like paint your nails and go to a disco." Such is life.

Teachers get very excited if you like reading too and swarm around getting you to read aloud and compare Harry Potter to Frodo Baggins and all this, and talk about plots and stuff which ruins reading really, as it is something you should just get lost in as far as I am concerned and not have to go on and on about as if you were on the radio or something. But don't get me wrong, I LOVE reading, especially books about people like me – hah!

RELIGION

RE is quite fun at school 'cos we do all the festivals and get to make cards for Diwali, Hannukah, Easter and all, whatever.

Unfortunately, all these nice sounding religious people seem to be quite keen to fight each other out there in the real world. Maybe they think they're all going to go to Heaven, so it doesn't matter. Me, I'm not so sure. What would Heaven be like? Would there be people there from other planets? Would there be animals there or would Harpo go to a Great Kennel in the Sky instead? Would you be in the same clothes you died in forever? What would you DO all day? And how bad would you have to be to go to Hell?

RUDE NOISES

Cats fart
Bats fart
Old men in
hats fart.

Dogs fart
Hogs fart

Little frogs on
logs fart.

People wearing jeans fart
People dressed in green fart
People eating beans fart
Even Kings and Queens fart.

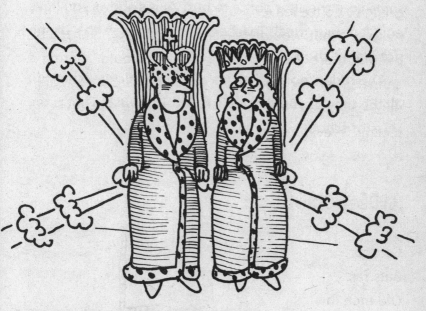

Teachers have been known to fart
when telling children off.
But don't say 'fart' in front of them
(they call it 'bottom cough').

Yes, folks, everyone does it sometimes! And, if you're a vegetarian like me, you probably do it lots! So don't worry about it. If poss, try to do it near a dog, then you can blame the dog... or even better, a horse. It's not quite so easy to blame a hamster or a goldfish... (**See Pets**)

Burping, or belching, is less rude than farting and in some countries it is polite to burp 'cos it shows you have enjoyed your meal. Teachers and aunties in the UK do not like it, though.

The rudest noise of all is shouting, which teachers do all the time. If you shout back: BIG TROUBLE. That is the rules of school.

S

SCHOOL

There are lots of different kinds of schools in the world, all of them are supposed to make you grow up into a 'good citizen'. It seems a pretty dumb idea to me to coop healthy young minds and bodies up in classrooms all day except for brief 'playtimes' when we are all turned out into a concrete thingy called a 'playground' and supposed to have fun. Eh? Ask your teacher if she would like to freeze in a concrete playground with two hundred other teachers for half an hour at a time? Especially with just one horrible foam football that you can't even kick properly, or a climbing frame that you can only use ONCE A WEEK and you're not allowed to SWING ON. Go on. Ask if you dare.

And some parents actually pay money to send their offsprings to these places! At some of THESE schools, when you're as young as seven years old, you actually have to stay the NIGHT. Every SINGLE night. I am Very Extremely pleased my parents are fond enough of me not to do that.

No offence, if your parents have sent you to boarding school, they might be nice people who are fond of you, but just very busy. Ask them. If your family is one of these mad (no offence) families, why not ask them how much it costs? Then work out how much this would be for your whole school life and ask them if you could go to ordinary school and have the money instead. I bet you it would be a massive amount of dosh.

People who go to schools where you have to pay, often end up running the country and then complaining about teachers and kids in ordinary schools. I say, take a look at the mess you are making and leave it to us ordinary folk to run our lives, so nah.

Trixie Tempest's plan for schools goes something like this: Make sure everyone learns to read, write, count to twenty (once you've done that you can get to infinity, I'm told). This should take about one hour each day. Then there should be lots of little spaces for FREE TIME: a sweety corner, a TV tunnel, an adventure playground, a football pitch with a proper ball and two goals, a book room, a dressing up room, a cookery room with sweety recipes as wallpaper, a music room, an art room, a drama room, a disco. Walls would be decorated with interesting Geography/History /Language facts (and I mean interesting facts like who invented the potato chip and whether it is true that football started by someone kicking an enemy's severed head) as well as great old paintings and poems and all, whatever.

Trixie Tempest's tips for enjoying school:
Have a book you like reading with you at all times. Slip it inside the book you are supposed to be reading.

Ask your teacher one of the following questions once a week (not more, else she will think you are trouble):

You look terrific! Have you had a face lift?

What is the speed of dark?

Why isn't phonetic spelt the way it sounds?

Now that we've calculators do we really need times tables?

If people from Poland are called Poles, are people from Holland called Holes?

Was it you my gran saw at Weight Watchers?

Did you know that if you weigh 300lb on Earth, on

Sirius B you would weigh 76,000 tons? Do you think they have Weight Watchers there?

Is there life on Uranus?

What was the naughtiest thing YOU ever did at school?

See also Exams, Teachers

SCHOOL TRIPS

These were always scary for me in Infants because I always thought I would get lost. Everyone else's mums or dads or carers used to come to at least one school trip a year, but mine never did (and still don't) because of work. But I won't want them to come when I am in Year Six, because the activity trip means being away from home for one whole week. Just think, seven days (and nights) without parents – yeah! I hope Harpo and Bonzo will remember me when I get back.

It is no fun if you don't like school trips when everyone else does. Also when you have to do Very Extremely boring things like going to graveyards and churches and taking rubbings off bits of old ruins. But Sumil and Dennis liked the graveyard as it gave them lots of chances to jump out from behind gravestones and

make Soppy Poppy scream. (Soppy Poppy will scream if you say hello, so she's quite fun to scare.)

Trixie Tempest tips on how to make school trips fun:

Art Gallery
Admire the fire extinguishers. Exclaim at their beautiful shape and colour.

Apologise loudly to the attendant for mistaking him for a sculpture.

Natural History Museums
Prepare a few labels (on computer) before you go and take some old toys (not your favourite teddy, obviously, just some old ones you don't like any more, or

something of your brother's, heh, heh). Place toys around exhibition with suitable labels, like 'Fluffykins – Neanderthal glove puppet, 2000 BC,' or 'Spiderman – the Missing Link,' or 'Space Barbie – thought to have landed on Earth two billion years ago and the mother of those we now know as Americans.'

Waxworks

Talk to the waxworks and watch people's reactions. Have big argument with the Prime Minister's waxwork, demanding Children's Rights. Tell everyone he doesn't seem to be listening. Make sure you get your photo taken with David Beckham. Then you can kid people it's a real pic.

Zoo

Talk very loudly about how small the cages are and how animals should be allowed to roam free. Ask the elephant keeper if he has a house which is exactly the same size as him. Talk seriously to the monkeys and listen, as if you can understand them. Talk to the snakes. Younger children will think you can speak parseltongue. Bang on the snake's window (just in case you are the next Harry Potter).

SLEEPOVERS

To make these worry free, just follow Trixie Tempest's sound advice and equip yourself with the 'Sleepovers made easy' starter kit.

Here is what is in it:

- Cool pyjamas
- Cool nail varnish set containing forty-two rainbow colours ('cos someone always wants to do nails) OR horror vampire face painting kit
- Fantastically scary video that you have watched six times over to make sure it doesn't scare YOU any more
- Note from your mum, dad or carer to be produced in emergency saying something like:

Please ensure my son/daughter is not exposed to scary videos as she/he turns into an axe murderer on such occasions and might murder one of the other children.

You only need to use this if someone is showing an even more scary video than the one you have, and you don't like it.

- Stuart Little, or similar, video cover box to put your scary video in
- Sleeping bag
- Teddy (If a boy, check out the teddy situation.

Some ten-year-old boys would not be seen dead or alive with a cuddly toy. Girls are lucky and go on having them in their teens... whoopeee!)

- **Pack of cards** for gambling
- **Very Extremely big bag of sweeties** (for gambling... and eating)

See also Bedwetting, Dark, Vampires, Zombies

SNOW

Campaign for schools to stop all lessons if there is enough snow to snowball. All day should be spent in the playground. Teachers should expect to be hit by at least six snowballs an hour. If you get a snowball down your neck, do not cry, it is weedy.

If your school has not obeyed the above instructions and if, while you are gazing longingly out of the window at the beautiful flakes of whispery whiteness softly falling out of your reach, your teacher tells you to pay attention, say the following:

"Are you not aware that snow, rare and beautiful, is Nature's natural plaything, put there for the peace and harmony of child and grown-up alike? And are you not aware that it is a natural urge of every child and grown-up to grab great big handfuls of it and toss it around? And are you not aware that building snowmen is a healthy way for children and grown-ups to learn how to work and play together? And a lesson that nothing in this life lasts forever and that we should take Nature's bounty when she offers it? And won't you please join in Trixie Tempest's campaign for a snowman in every playground? And can we borrow your coat/ hat/glassses/scarf to decorate it with?"

Please write to me and tell me how you get on.

STRANGER DANGER

When PC Toecap came in, he told us all the following, so I'm repeating it for those of you who weren't there.

"Always walk or cycle with a friend, never alone. Know the way you're going before you start. Stay away from empty buildings and unsafe places. Never take anything from a stranger. If a stranger asks you a question, don't talk. Run away. Don't go anywhere with a stranger. Tell a grown-up you trust if you see someone you think doesn't belong hanging around public rest rooms, playgrounds, or school yards. Follow these tips and you are on your way to staying safe."

Easier said than done, if you have just broken up with your BF and she won't walk home with you. And what is an unsafe place? Bottomley High Street, if the disgustrous driving is anything to go by. And what exactly IS a stranger? Is it anyone you don't know? Like a new postman asking if you'll take a parcel for next door? Still, Better Safe Than Sorry, as Grandma Clump would say. Or, Run Like Hell If You Feel Dodgy, as Trixie Tempest does say.

See also Home Alone

STOMACH ACHE

Usually caused by Schoolitis. Everyone needs a day off sometimes and tummy ache is usually the best way to convince your folks. You could heat the thermometer up a bit (careful not to do it too much else they will rush you to hospital), or put a bit of talcum powder on your cheeks to look pale and sickly. Other causes of tummy ache are:

Pains from gas caused by (sorry) drinking a lot of fizzy drinks.

Too much food.

Other kinds of indigestion.

What Grandma Clump calls 'The Time of the Month', and Grandma Tempest calls 'The Curse'. This hasn't happened to me yet, but some girls in Year Six already get these tummy aches.

Tummy aches don't usually last long so if you want a week off school you'll have to act really well.

SWIMMING

Femka is scarily good at swimming – I think she has webbed toes, 'cos she always wears little rubber socks in the swimming pool, but maybe that's for verrucas. But I am almost scarily good too, and I am going to beat Femka if it's the last thing I do. There are still quite a lot of people in my class who cannot swim, that's because we don't start swimming at St Aubergine's until Year Five, which I think is daft because we could all drown! I think schools should teach important things like life-saving and first aid and cycling and how to dial

999 and LIFE SKILLS from the first year of Juniors. Of course, kids like me with teachers for mums and two parents and enough money all get swimming lessons from when we are babies and that is why I am scarily good at swimming, so it's not your fault if you're not.

If only our local pool looked like this.

It is a bit boring diving in to save the life of a brick, though. I think we should practise with something a bit more exciting... David Beckham, perhaps... or Gareth Gates?

Ever seen a stick-insect rescuing a brick?

T

TATTOOS

Orange Orson has a real tattoo! And he is only eleven. It is of a skull, on his bum! I know, 'cos he showed Sumil and Sumil told me. I bet the teachers don't know but if he tries to stick my head down the toilet one more time I think I am going to drop a hint. Maybe he will get expelled. But then of course he would go off to a prison school or something and learn evil ways, which he is pretty good at learning already.

TEACHERS

There are two kinds of teachers:
A) Kind and B) Not Kind.

In our school, all the Reception and Infant teachers, especially Mrs Cluck and Mrs Soothe, who look after the Reception classes are Type A. All the Junior teachers are Type B. At least, that's what I thought before our usual teacher, Miss Took, went off sick. Then we had our supply teacher, Warty-Beak, who I think is type Z. I now realise that Miss Took was heaven-in-a-basket compared to Warty-Beak.

Here is a picture of Warty-Beak in a Very Extremely good mood. I think you have now got my point.

Teacher A   B   Arrrrg!

Kindly Type A teachers come in three main sorts:

Cuddly

Usually old, with soft jumpers. It is not Very Extremely easy to go home with a tummy ache if your teacher is cuddly, because she will be so kind you will forget you are feeling upset.

Bouncy

Young, and mainly from Australia, Canada, or New Zealand. Bouncy teachers have loads of songs and stories about kookaburras and love telling you about their life on the open plain. If you are lucky, they will bring in a guitar and you can spend all day singing. They give lots of stars and "Trixie did some careful work today, give her a pat on the back" stickers. If you have a bouncy teacher, your class will be happy.

Dreamy

Fun, because they are forgetful.

"No, Mrs Daffy, you did not ask us to copy out our work in best, and that is why we haven't done it."

"Silly me. Will you all do it for next week then?"

"Of course we will, Mrs Daffy."

"Lovely."

But next week never comes.

Unkindly Type B teachers come in two main sorts:

Shouting

Can be young or old and, confusingly, can have soft jumpers. Their classes are always Very Extremely naughty, because they get shouted at all the time whether they are naughty or not, so it is more fun to be shouted at and naughty than shouted at and good.

158

There are always some very sad quiet children at the back of these classes who have no idea what is going on as they have shut their ears down. I want to say to these teachers: "Have you been shouted at recently? Maybe by a rude driver? Or a policeman or something? And did you LIKE it? Or did it make you feel really bad and really SMALL?"

I think they would agree it made them feel really bad. But they don't seem to understand that the same goes for us kids. Shouting teachers don't get any respect, because they don't give any. Paste this on your teacher's wall, if you dare.

Sarcastic
These teachers give up very quickly.

"Oh, I see, no one wants to learn anything today. We'll all just sit here then. It's you who are the losers..." and on and on. Drone drone.

Trixie Tempest's tips for coping with teachers:
Try to encourage your teacher to teach well. He or she should arrive on time, with work prepared and lots of interesting things to tell you. He or she should allow you to go to the loo so you don't wee on the carpet.

(It's amazing how often teachers allow small kids to do that and it is no fun for the kids, or the teachers, or the carpet.) He or she must be good at reading stories and doing all the voices, give him or her a demonstration, if necessary.

Always offer to help the teacher. Nice ones deserve it, nasty ones might get off your case.

See also Schools

TEETH
See Dentist

TRAINERS
I have pink trainers and blue trainers. The only person, in my opinion, who should wear white shoes is David Beckham (my HERO). So there. I like to customise my trainers with shoe dye. It is quite easy to paint pictures on them and they last quite well. Also, you can do it with Very Extremely cheap trainers and no one can tell. In fact, you can pretend they are Very Extremely expensive ones that have been flown over from New York. Grey Griselda and her gang did not believe me when I said this and said why would posh New

York or Paris designers paint pictures that look like they had been done by a five-year-old with a learning disability.

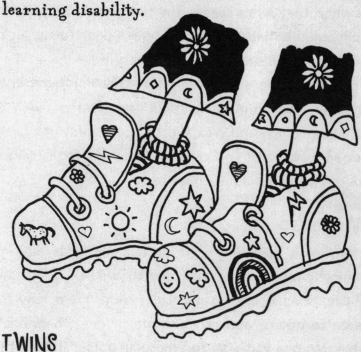

TWINS

I think it would be great to be a twin because you could always pretend to be the other one. That is what Wax and Bugsy in our year do. Wax is in my class and Bugsy is in Mrs Bottle's class. But quite often (about four times a term) they swap, so Bugsy is in our class and Wax is in Mrs Bottle's class. And the teachers never notice!! All the kids know, of course, but we kids never tell. I think that would be the best fun. Wax is always Very Extremely naughty and Bugsy is Very Extremely good. So when they swap classes, the teacher always says, "I don't know what's come over Wax/Bugsy today. He's usually so good/such a handful." Heh! Heh!

The downside, says Wax, is they often only get one birthday card from their folks and aunties. HAPPY BIRTHDAY Bugsy and Wax. Worse, there's only one fiver pinned inside and you can't get peanuts for £2.50 in this day and age. But such is life.

TV

Television is *remarkably* educational and has a Very Extremely useful role in teaching children the Meaning of Life. Soap operas in particular show them how to relate to others, and cartoons are of *great* beneficial value. Wall-to-wall TV (for those that like it) can be particularly educational for those in the 7-11 age group.

There, I have taken a lot of time and trouble making that sound Very Extremely grown-up as though it was written by a Televisionologist. So I hope you will photocopy it and stick it in front of your parents' noses. (*See also Cartoons*)

Naturally, I only watch a few things myself, mainly

'cos I have to keep up with playground gossip. *Vera the Veggie Vampire* is everyone's Big Thing at the moment, but I get driven a bit nuts by Dinah, who does every episode and all the voices the next day, so it's a bit like having to watch it twice.

U

UNUSUAL

If you're worried about being unusual, remember that everyone is unusual. It is unusual to play the trumpet at ten (specially with a baby tooth in the front row). It is

unusual to be as small and round as Tomato. It is unusual to be good at doing voices, like Dinah. It is unusual to be able to eat sweets all day without being sick, like Chloe. It is unusual to be twins, like Bugsy and Wax. So if you think you and your family are unusual, that is a Very Extremely good thing.

UGLY

If you are worried about being ugly, I bet you are not. Children are *never* ugly. And if someone tells you you are ugly, it is probably because they think they are, so they need to pretend someone is uglier than them. TAKE NO NOTICE and tell your self every day that you are GORGEOUS!

V

VAMPIRES

Vampires are big on TV thanks to *Buffy the Vampire Slayer* and *Vera the Veggie Vampire*, who everyone in my class watches. Real vampires suck your blood though and the most famous one is Count Dracula. Count Dracula was born in Transylvania in 1471. He is still alive, being one of the great Undead, and comes at dead of night to drink your blood. He sleeps in a coffin and has bat wings and fangs. He looks

handsome if he wants to get to know you. Luckily, he has never been seen in Bottomley, but I keep my window closed at night just in case. Dracula is not someone you should think about before going to sleep, if poss.

See also Dreams (and Nightmares)

VIOLENCE

There is a lot on television about footballers and TV stars who beat up their wives. If this is going on in your house, you really should get help. And if your mum or dad hits you, you must get help. And just because they aren't actually hitting you, doesn't mean they aren't hurting you. Name calling and shouting is violence too, but it is harder to prove. There are families where all the kids are treated fine except one. There was one where the youngest child was kept in a chicken coop, while everyone else was happy. This is scary stuff, but if you know anyone who is being terribly treated like this, or if you are yourself, it is Very Extremely important to get help. If you don't want to talk to someone you know, like a teacher, you can call Childline on 0800 1111. DO NOT SUFFER IN SILENCE. GET HELP.

VOICE

(This should really be A for Accents, but I had enough As and not enough Vs!)

If you move from London to Yorkshire your voice will start to sound different before long.

Why? Because if you talk like The Queen everyone else will think you are posh. After *thinking* you are posh (about half a zygo-second later, according to Tearaway Tempest's time-machine calculator) they will *say* you are posh, and they probably won't say it very nicely. No point in saying, "We are all different, let us learn to celebrate and share our multitude of talents and individuality" and all, whatever, like the head teacher. **The bottom line is, talk like everyone else and you will FIT IN. Shame, isn't it?**

If, on the other hand, you talk like Eliza Dolittle in *My Fair Lady* while she is still selling the flowers, and then you get a scholarship to the St Sumptious Academy for Young Ladies, or Eton or somewhere if you are a boy, you are also going to change your accent. That's how accents work.

One thing you CAN do, is be nice to someone who you think speaks with a funny accent, or has a funny voice. Then at least YOU won't be one of the bullies.

Trixie's Burning Question:
Who was mean enough to put an 's' in the word 'lisp'?

WAR

I did a big poster for the last war which said:

> BLOODY war
>
> BLOODY war
>
> BLOODY war
>
> What is it for?

It was just big black letters with blood dripping off. Tomato thought that was swearing, which shows he does not know enough to be a member of the Kids' Parliament yet. But I have now watched about real war on television, and I know that those are real dead children.

I have noticed that most children are against war, but not most grown-ups. Do they know something we don't? What is the use of saying, "if someone hits you in the playground, don't hit back," when they go off and bomb children? In the last war my dad told me the army used things called cluster bombs which often lie about unexploded until a small child picks one up and blinds itself. Even children – especially children – can see this is wrong. I think it is up to us to teach grown-ups that wars are wrong. We are going to be the next lot of grown-ups and we want to be around long enough to prove that we CAN stop wars. If there are still wars in fifty years' time, it will be OUR fault as well. So start planning NOW. We have got to find out all we can about why wars start and do everything we can to stop it ever happening again.

WASPS

What are wasps for? It's easy to see what bees are for, but what is the point of wasps (apart from that stingy point)? Wasps love sweet things, like jam doughnuts all covered in lovely sugar, honey and all, whatever, so you could try giving those up!!! But this is not very likely if you have a sweet tooth like me. One thing I do know, wasps love PANIC. So if one comes near you, don't flap about and squeal, it will make it worse. If one lands on a window, you can quietly put a glass over it, then slide a postcard under the glass, and chuck it out of the open window. (The wasp, not the glass!) Or, if your dad is like mine, you can ask him to swat it with a newspaper – preferably one he has already read. And you can run away from wasps, but make sure you are not carrying a jam doughnut, or a honey spoon... as it will follow you.

See also Bee Stings

WEDDINGS

When I was six I begged and begged to go to my aunt's wedding. She was one of my witchy aunts on my dad's side of the family, and Mum and Dad kept saying no and making excuses and I thought they were being just like the Dursleys in Harry Potter. I stamped my little foot and shouted and screamed until they took pity on me and even bought me the dress I wanted, which was all spangles and stars and flowers and bows and frills and a lovely cream colour with just a hint of palest pink and I thought I looked like a fairy bride and I loved it to pieces (I WAS only six). But when I got to the wedding everyone else was in black, which is what they wear at witches' weddings, only I was too busy shouting and screaming to listen to my dad telling this. So I ended up looking like a potato in a scuttle.

They were very nice to me, in the way that people are, sometimes, to Very Extremely stupid people who don't know any better, but it has put me off weddings, a bit. Though I have begged and begged my parents to have a wedding, but they can't be bothered.

WHAT? (will you do when you are grown up... etc)

Salvia (yeh, I know her name nearly spells saliva, but she's cool) is a totally excellent dancer. At the last school play she did this amazing stuff on points and all this and some old dear said afterwards: "Are you going to be a dancer when you grow up?"

And Salvia said, "I already AM a dancer."

This is a very good reply, as who knows what on earth they want to do for the rest of their life when they're ten years old?

Here is a list of My Dream Jobs (you can write your list next to them if you like, as long as you haven't got this book from the library).

YOUR LIST

...timillionaire

...er of Harry Potter

...JK Rowling

...n't mind me

...the next one,

...probably tired out

...w)

...shmallow and

...y taster

- Jockey (I am small enough and I don't think a girl has won the Derby yet. That will be me!)
- Footballer (first girl to captain England)
- James Bond
- Trumpet playing pop star
- Professional snowman builder
- Theme-park ride tester
- Witch

Things I do NOT want to do:

- Butler
- Cleaner
- Ugly woman in freak show
- Sewage worker
- Cement mixer
- Boil lancer

Things you do NOT want to do:

- Home-improvement specialist
- Door to door duster seller
- Air hostess
- Ballerina

(Apologies to those of you who fancy the last two, but that sort of thing is not my bag and you would understand if you have seen me trying to do ballet or host a plane.)

WHINGEING

My own family is Very Extremely annoying in this respect as we all whinge a lot. Tomato whinges about food, mostly. He eats five tons of Krispy Popsickles and then whines for more. Mum says he's a Growing Boy and needs his food. She is right, but he is only growing outwards as far as I can see. Mum whinges about us not tidying anything up and how she has to do everything all the time. Dad whinges about Mum whingeing and says does she understand what it's like working for la-di-da ladies who want all their rooms painted white and then decide it's the wrong kind of white and all this? And I am as you know, Very Extremely put upon having such a whingeing Dad, Mum and brother. However, I do know that whingeing is Very Extremely unattractive and doesn't always get you what you want, which is why I NEVER whinge for a horse!

WITCHES

My family on Dad's side are all witches, but because Mum's isn't, I might NOT be a witch when I grow up. I am still waiting for that letter from Hogwarts, but maybe it will come in a year, when I'm in Year Six. The reason I started trumpet was that all the girls on the witchy side of the family played a musical instrument. There was Great-Great-Great Aunt Zoe, who was a Highland harpist, famous for luring wicked barons into her castle and then hypnotising them with her harp to give away

all their land to the poor. And there was Zarabeena, who played the zither, so they say, for Gandalf himself whenever he was in Scotland – where apparently he often fled to get away from Hobbits. Then there was Zachary whose violin was so sweet that the birds used to fly in for music lessons.

So I reckoned I needed to keep up the tradition in case I got to be a witch one day. Fat chance, as my mum's side of the family, the Clumps, are about as magical as Brussels sprouts.

XMAS

If you are from a Muslim or Jewish family, or another religion, you probably don't celebrate Christmas... but then you have lots of other Very Extremely nice festivals instead. To some grown-ups, Christmas is all about carols and vicars. Our family is mixed. The witchy side don't bother with Christmas at all. Grandma Tempest goes to a big Pagan Festival at New Year. But Grandma Clump likes to go and sing *Away in a Manger*, and even watches the Queen on TV on Christmas Day. She is usually asleep by the time Queenie comes on, but I think that is because by then she has drunk too much 'toddy'. She says 'toddy' is ginger beer and lemonade, but it smells like BOOOZE to me. I love Christmas. What is nicer than a Christmas tree? Or a big fat Christmas stocking? Or a big fat pile of prezzies? I like the fact that we all give each other something at

Christmas, which makes it like lots of birthdays all rolled together. And I like the fact that we don't do anything on Christmas Day except Christmassy stuff. Soon I shall make a Big Invention which will be a nut roast that tastes like turkey, because even though I am a vegetarian, I am sorry to say that I have been known to eat turkey on Christmas Day. **Sorry to any turkeys who are reading this, and to other vegetarians who do not give in at Christmas, but rules are sometimes made to be broken. At least, mine are.**

y

yo-yos

This was a Very Extremely big craze back when I was three years old and I kidyounot, I was the very first yo-yoing two-year-old. I could yo-yo better than I could talk. It was dying down a bit by the time I got to nursery, but I can still do a mean yo-yo with all the moves and it is still worth taking the old yo-yo to the playground to show off, if you ARE good at it. Like all crazes, this is Very Extremely fun if you have a natural talent at it like me (not to boast), and Very Extremely boring if you haven't.

See also Crazes

you

Remember, YOU are the most important person in your life, so you're worth thinking about.

1. Palominus
2. Pegasus
3. Harpissimus
4. Dalmat
5. Catimus
6. Felines

Here is my version of all the star signs. I think it rather lovely and a lot nicer than the boring ones you get in the comics.

Woofus

Monsterus

Boy Bandus

Girl Bandia

Merlino

Draw your own

Choose the one you like best. Then put your birthday month on it. Read your amazing character and horoscope on P. 184!

Palominus
Very kind, horse lover

You will live a long and happy life

Pegasus
You are very lovable

Your dreams will come true

Harpissimus
You are nice and like dogs

Your long life will be happy

Dalmatia
Clever dog lover

Your happy life will last ages

Catimus
Strong cat lover

Your wishes will be realised

Felines
Adventurous, fond of cats

Your fun-packed life will be long

Woofus
Wise, fond of dogs

You'll realise your ambitions

Monsterus
Helpful, fond of monsters

Health and happiness are yours

Boy Bandus
Sweet, music lover

You'll marry four pop stars

Girl Bandia
Sweet, music lover

Four pop stars will marry you

Merlino
Marvellous in every way

Everything good will come to you

Draw Your Own
Creative

You will make your own opportunities
and they will be superb

When you have chosen your own star sign, you can put all your friends and family in too. For example, if you are born in April and have chosen Harpissimus, and your Mum is born in May, then she will be Dalmatia. If your brother is born in September, then he will be Monsterus, geddit? This is more accurate than any other horoscope on Earth.

ZOMBIES

Zombies are the walking dead. I only know one, which is Warty-Beak. It worries me, though, as he is going to marry Ms Mortice, who is our quite nice assistant head teacher. She obviously does not know he is a zombie and I think she should be warned, otherwise she might end up with a whole family of baby zombies and they might take over the world...

See also Babies, Dreams (and Nightmares), Sleepovers, Vampires

Bye bye, sob sob, it is the end of my Very Extremely Brilliant Guide to Everything and now I keep thinking of all the wondrous and disgustrous things I have left out, like armadillos and toe rings and pirates, to name but a few.

If all pirates looked like Johnny Depp I would of course have included them.

But do send me a postcard if there's anything really important to YOU that I have left out and I can include it in the next edition.

See you in my next book.

Lots of love,

Trixie

(and HARPO and BONzo)

Oh, OK then, and TOmatO

x x x x x x x x x

USEFUL WEB ADDRESSES & PHONE NUMBERS

ChildLine   Freephone 0800 1111

Kidscape   www.kidscape.org.uk

R.S.P.B   www.rspb.org.uk
(Royal Society for the Protection of Birds)

R.S.P.C.A   www.rspca.org.uk
(Royal Society for the Protection of Animals)
Emergency line 0870 5555999

UKYP   www.ukyp.org.uk
(United Kingdom Youth Parliament)

Trixie

AND the Amazing Doggy Yap Star

ROS ASQUITH

Hi, it's me, Trixie!

This book is all about me and
my Very Extremely smart dog
Harpo. Ever since we got her,
she never made a sound.
But now she's an amazing talking,
singing, yap-artist!

Join us on our mega money-making
adventure...

www.harpercollinschildrensbooks.co.uk

extract from Trixie and the Amazing Doggy Yap Star

It started this morning before breakfast. Harpo was helping out, as usual. She is a sleepy kind of pooch most of the time, and I don't deny she is on the plump side – well, fat, really – but she is also Very Extremely clever for a dog, and very extraordinarily good at stuff dogs do in books but hardly ever do in real life, like fetching slippers and the morning paper.

This morning she was fetching the slippers and she came in with only one.

"Where's Dad's other slipper?" I asked her, expecting her to go back and look for it.

And she looked up really high, pointing her nose right up as if peering into a Far Distant Universe where the planets were made only of Fidoburgers and she went: "WOOF."

Now you could say, that's just the noise dogs make, but she'd never made it before, so for her it was a miracle. And there was something about the way she kept staring upwards as she made it. It couldn't possibly be, I thought to myself, that she's trying to say "roof" could it?

I decided to get really sneaky.

"What's the brown stuff around the outside of the tree trunks you wee against?"

"Bark," she said, clear as clear.

Then the fireworks started going off in my brain. A PLAN was taking shape – a plan to make ALL my dreams come true...

Trixie

AND the DREAM PONY OF DOOM

ROS ASQUITH

Hi, Trixie here!

Did you know that the thing I've always wanted most in the world is a pony? It's my biggest wish and dreamiest dream!

And did you ever hear the words, "Be careful what you wish for, it might come true"? It's the sort of thing my Grandma Clump says.

No, I didn't understand either. But I do now...!

www.harpercollinschildrensbooks.co.uk

extract from Trixie and the Dream Pony of Doom

I pulled out my £250 cash and before I knew it, Bullet Head had whipped it out of my hand to count it, which he did in a blur, like someone who is used to counting Very Extremely Large amounts of money. I felt my heart miss a beat. Then he said, "Pony's out the back," and it missed a beat again.

The door slammed shut and the bolts clanged into place.

"But we don't know anything about it! How old is it? What's its NAME?" shouted Dinah, aiming a ferocious kick at the door.

Chloe pushed her before she could land the kick. "Don't," she hissed. "He could murder us."

This seemed like wise advice even to the furious Dinah. "But there probably isn't even a pony there," she grumbled.

"Fungus," came a voice from behind the door.

"What?"

My stomach was somersaulting. I knew there would be no pony. Maybe there would be an army of Rottweilers... But these thoughts only coursed through my brain for a couple of seconds because then I got my first sight of Fungus, my Dream Pony...